Bridging the WASH
Humanitarian–Development Divide

Praise for this book

'The book is a "must-read" for those working in the humanitarian and development sectors, in the field of WASH and beyond. The rich compilation of lessons learned, case studies, and conversations from a diverse array of WASH experts provides valuable insight on the humanitarian and development divide and the future of the WASH sector.'

Monica Ramos, Global WASH Cluster Coordinator, UNICEF

'Ongoing conflicts and complex humanitarian situations around the globe mean the average length of protracted refugee situations now exceeds twenty years. Away from home, refugees and internally displaced people are among the most vulnerable and disadvantaged groups, often denied access to basic water supply and sanitation services, and at risk of being "left behind" as the world strives to achieve the Sustainable Development Goal 6 target of safe drinking water and sanitation for all. It is therefore more important than ever to grapple with the challenge of bridging the WASH humanitarian–development divide to ensure refugees do not remain dependent recipients of unsustainable humanitarian aid. Rather, the focus must be on enabling refugee self-reliance and including refugees in sustainable development programmes for provision of equitable WASH services.

'*Bridging the WASH Humanitarian–Development Divide* is a welcome contribution, providing insights and guidance for one of the most complex issues that the world must overcome to ensure no one is left behind as we strive together to achieve the UN Sustainable Development Goals.'

Murray Burt, Chief Engineer at Auckland Transport (New Zealand Government); former UNHCR HQ Global Senior WASH Officer

'An important contribution to moving forward the WASH humanitarian–development–peace nexus agenda, especially from the humanitarian perspective.'

Tim Grieve, senior consultant, water, sanitation, and public health; former UNICEF HQ Senior Advisor – Emergency Water, Sanitation, and Hygiene

Bridging the WASH Humanitarian–Development Divide

Building a sustainable reality

Mariëlle Snel and Nikolas Sorensen

Practical
ACTION
PUBLISHING

Practical Action Publishing Ltd
27a Albert Street, Rugby, CV21 2SG, UK
www.practicalactionpublishing.com

A catalogue record for this book is available from the British Library.

A catalogue record for this book has been requested from the Library of Congress.

ISBN 978-1-78853-173-3 Paperback
ISBN 978-1-78853-174-0 Hardback
ISBN 978-1-78853-176-4 eBook

Citation: Snel, M. and Sorensen, N. (2021) *Bridging the WASH Humanitarian–Development Divide: Building a sustainable reality*, Rugby, UK: Practical Action Publishing <http://dx.doi.org/10.3362/9781788531764>.

Since 1974, Practical Action Publishing has published and disseminated books and information in support of international development work throughout the world. Practical Action Publishing is a trading name of Practical Action Publishing Ltd (Company Reg. No. 1159018), the wholly owned publishing company of Practical Action. Practical Action Publishing trades only in support of its parent charity objectives and any profits are covenanted back to Practical Action (Charity Reg. No. 247257, Group VAT Registration No. 880 9924 76).

Cover photo: Bridge near Korek mountain in Kurdish region of Iraq
Photo credit: Michael Wicker
Typeset by vPrompt eServices, India

Contents

Boxes and figures

Boxes

Figures

Acronyms

A4EP	Alliance for Empowering Partnership
BASICS	bold action to stop infections in clinical settings
CFUs	colony-forming units
CHAST	child hygiene and sanitation training
CHP	clean household approach
CLTS	community-led total sanitation
CONCORD	Confederation for Cooperation of Relief and Development NGOs
DRR	disaster risk reduction
ECHO	European Civil Protection and Humanitarian Aid Operations
FAO	Food and Agriculture Organization of the United Nations
FGDs	field group discussions
FIETS	financial, institutional, environmental, technological, and social
FRC	free residual chlorine
GWC	Global WASH Cluster
HFV	haemorrhagic fever virus
HPMs	handpump mechanics
IASC	Inter-Agency Standing Committee
ICRC	International Committee of the Red Cross
ICVA	International Council of Voluntary Agencies
IEC	information, education, and communication
INGOs	international non-government organizations
IOM	International Organization for Migration
IPC	infection, prevention, and control
IRC	International Water and Sanitation Centre
KAP	knowledge, attitudes, and practices
MHM	menstrual hygiene management
NTU	nephelometric turbidity units
OCHA	United Nations Office for the Coordination of Humanitarian Affairs
ODI	Overseas Development Institute
OECD	Organisation for Economic Co-operation and Development
PDM	post-distribution monitoring
PE	polyethylene
PHAST	participatory hygiene and sanitation transformation
PLWD	people living with disabilities
PPE	personal protective equipment
SAM	severe acute malnutrition
SARS	severe acute respiratory syndrome

SDG	Sustainable Development Goal
SNV	Netherlands Development Organization
SODIS	solar disinfection
SWA	Sanitation and Water for All
UD	urine diversion
UNHCR	United Nations High Commissioner for Refugees (UN Refugee Agency)
UNICEF	United Nations Children's Fund
VOICE	Voluntary Organisation in Cooperation in Emergencies
WASH	water, sanitation, and hygiene
WEDC	Water, Engineering and Development Centre
WHO	World Health Organization

Acknowledgements

We are tremendously grateful for the numerous people that have helped make this book possible. Although we cannot thank everyone here by name, we do want to give special thanks to Umar Bishara, Omeed Enwiya, Peter Nyamoko, and Thaw Si Htin Zaw at Save the Children and Hasmik Hocharyan, Rosanna Keam, and Michael Wicker at World Vision. Their knowledge made our case studies possible. Additionally, we want to thank the various WASH professionals who participated through survey and by interview for their time and expertise; this book would not have been complete without their vital input. We also want to thank Toby Gould for his keen revisions and suggestions. We are also grateful for the professional and dedicated assistance received from all the staff at Practical Action Publishing, with special thanks to Jenny Peebles, Clare Tawney, Kelly Somers, and Rosanna Denning.

As always, this book would not be possible without the support of our amazing families: Erin, Xander, Piet, Nel, Isabelle, Job, and Mathilde, whose encouragement and understanding was immeasurably felt.

CHAPTER 1
Introduction

The provision of safe water, sanitation, and hygiene (WASH) is essential to protecting human health and providing the necessary environment in which people can develop and maintain livelihoods. This is especially true in humanitarian crises. Safe access to WASH services is often disrupted for long periods of time, leading to illness, death, and loss of opportunity. Humanitarian crises are become increasingly complicated, as responders have to negotiate the consequences of conflict and climate change. When this book was being written, there were an estimated 235 million people requiring humanitarian assistance worldwide (OCHA, 2020a), and this number continues to grow. The outcomes of WASH development programmes are also becoming more fragile and are sensitive to destabilizing forces, especially climate change. As new emergencies have been added to the growing list of needs already addressed by humanitarian responders, organizations have rapidly expanded their operations to meet them. This has posed challenges for humanitarian organizations as they attempt to meet increasingly prolonged emergencies, often lasting years (Guinote, 2018). When emergencies last several years, there is a tension between meeting the needs of newly affected people and addressing the longer-term needs of people who fled the conflict years earlier, which can result in a 'continual emergency programme'. With the average humanitarian crisis growing in length (Nakamitsu et al., 2017), we argue here, as we did in a previous publication, that 'relief response can no longer be viewed merely through the humanitarian lens, but current and future crisis responses increasingly require long-term development considerations' (Sorensen and Snel, 2020: 278). How do we develop effective humanitarian WASH programming that keeps long-term development goals in mind?

Disaster risk reduction is an area where there is confusion about the roles of development and humanitarian practitioners. Humanitarian WASH actors often identify disaster risk reduction activities and programmes during the transition period, but they focus on government policy, community action, and long-term programme outcomes. Disaster risk reduction is often addressed more effectively as a development programme or as a shared responsibility between humanitarian and development actors, with humanitarians aware of the risks and development actors defining and implementing the long-term planning objectives. Climate change adaptation is also an area that benefits from clear collaboration, and so both humanitarian and development actors should be engaged.

Humanitarian and development actors will all be working with the same government ministries, local authorities, and utility providers, sometimes in different geographical locations (camps versus towns) but often in the same places. These actors will have different timeframes, goals, and unique donors that impose conflicting conditions on their funding. For the authorities, humanitarian and development actors can be seen as confusing, with misaligned goals often set against each other. Humanitarians can be seen by the authorities as not understanding the realities of the situation and as making unrealistic demands. As the newcomer, it should be the role of the humanitarian actor to engage wherever possible with the development plans of the authorities and utility providers; to at least 'do no harm' to existing plans; and, where feasible, to align humanitarian short-term plans with the authorities' long-term strategy.

In this publication, we utilize examples of WASH programming implemented in humanitarian settings. We aim to address the 'how' question and discuss lessons learned in bridging the humanitarian, development, and peace nexus, with a particular focus on the humanitarian and development divide. This book shares some of the experiences and key lessons learned in the WASH sector in various countries across Africa, Asia, and the Middle East, with the aim of providing a call to action that will inspire humanitarian, development, and government professionals, in and outside the sector, to improve the long-term impact of sustainable WASH programmes in humanitarian contexts. However, this publication does not provide a silver bullet solution to the WASH sector's most pressing challenges; rather, it offers reflections on the field's most recent developments.

In our discussion, we draw on case studies from the field and conversations with WASH thinkers and programme designers to reflect on the WASH humanitarian, development, and peace nexus and the WASH sector's future, including who future WASH professionals will be. Our research included insights from WASH professionals and thinkers, collected through a survey conducted between May and June 2020,[1] and open-ended interviews conducted from June 2020 to February 2021.[2] Our discussion here is designed to be a continuation of an ongoing debate around sustainable WASH services in humanitarian settings and the triple nexus; it is part of conversations including the 'Triple Nexus in WASH'[3] meeting that took place in February 2021, which aimed to create stronger synergy between humanitarian and development WASH actors. This meeting brought both humanitarian and development WASH professionals to the table and reflects the importance of the ongoing conversation and the need to continue debates around WASH sustainability, resilience, and minimizing harm ('do no harm') that are aligned with platforms for peace.

The primary audience for this publication is professionals working in the humanitarian and development WASH sector, but we hope that it will be of interest to others across the humanitarian, development, and peace sectors, ranging from government officials to managers working directly or indirectly around WASH, especially in the area of public health. This fundamental curiosity was based on our own observations in the field, on speaking with other humanitarian and development professionals, and on reflections on existing field, practical, and academic literature.

Our crucial questions focus on how sustainable WASH services can – or should – occur across the humanitarian and development WASH spectrum and on the role governments, international non-government organizations (INGOs), and other thinkers play in improving such services. To answer this question, we rely on current WASH literature, surveys, and interviews with a range of humanitarian and development WASH professionals, as well as several country case studies from Africa, Asia, and the Middle East. There is also a focus on utilizing the sustainable WASH model as a lens in our discussions.

Before moving on, a brief note on definitions is needed. There are still inconsistencies between the humanitarian and development sectors and their use of terms. Box 1.1 therefore provides a few key definitions of terms as they are used throughout this book.

Box 1.1 Definitions

Fragile: The German WASH Network states:

> A uniform definition of fragility does not exist. Fragile countries are charac-terised by serious deficiencies in at least one of the following three dimensions: capacity (the state lacks capability to provide basic public services), legitimacy and authority. Three important country list [sic] have prevailed (OECD 'Fragile State List'; World Bank 'Harmonised List of Fragile Situations'; Fund for Peace 'Fragile States Index'). All three list are based on the three dimensions, but they use different sources of information and differently weighted indicators, using different sub-categories to arrive to overall evaluations, which rely on different threshold values for dividing countries in fragility classes. The results vary consid-erably. Since the OECD uses the broadest definition of fragility, its list is also the most comprehensive (56 countries). What is striking is that only 18 countries were considered 'fragile' in 2017 according to all three definitions/lists. (German WASH Network, 2019: 5).

Integrated WASH: This focuses on the nexus between WASH and nutrition, education, livelihoods, child protection, agriculture, and food security. The integrated WASH approach enables more people to gain access to improved services, including humanitarian, transi-tional, and longer-term WASH.

Sustainable WASH model: This reflects not only on the technical aspects involved in WASH, but also on the environmental, institutional, financial, and socio-cultural aspects.

The Humanitarian Development Peace Nexus: This refers to an ongoing discussion about the intersection between the humanitarian, development, and peace sectors and how humanitarian, development, and governmental organizations and institutions work – or don't work – together to solve pressing problems. The main focus of this book is on

---

(Continued)

Box 1.1 Continued

the humanitarian sector and how best to link it to development and peace considerations. We also use the terms 'divide' and 'spectrum' interchangeably with the term 'nexus'. The terms 'humanitarian' and 'development' are also used to denote contexts or phases along a spectrum, moving from the start of an emergency through a transitional phase and into long-term development. The 'peace' element, often referred to as 'governance' or 'government', is not an explicit phase on the spectrum; rather, it is an institutional requirement for the long-term success of WASH interventions. Often, in humanitarian contexts, government institutions are weak or weakened, and as international development programmes move forward, the ideal outcome is for government institutions (or communities) to adopt and maintain WASH infrastructure as the priority of humanitarian and development organizations shifts to new emergencies.

COVID-19 and recent WASH developments

In recent months, as we have been developing this book, the COVID-19 pandemic has started to alter the role WASH plays in humanitarian and development settings. WASH is vital to successful pandemic response, as safe water, sanitation, and hygienic conditions are fundamental in protecting human health during any infectious disease outbreak. COVID-19 has become the first extreme pandemic the world has experienced in over a century. As described by Howard et al.:

> COVID-19 is only the most recent emerging infectious disease with pandemic potential. Concerns over pandemics since the 1800s provided an impetus for the development of the science of public health and systems of international governance of public health – a history in WaSH has played important and at times foundational roles. The pandemic highlights that adequate hygiene and access to safe and reliable water and sanitation are essential to preparedness, prevention and response; as well as protecting human life at other times. (Howard et al., 2020: 625)

As the COVID-19 pandemic is ongoing, its full impact on the humanitarian and development WASH sector is still unclear. However, the COVID-19 outbreak has clearly had a significant effect on the entire globe, impacting the day-to-day lives of millions of people worldwide, further blurring the lines between humanitarian and development silos, and bringing humanitarian considerations into every development context.

The current humanitarian setting

With emergency contexts lasting for longer periods of time, during the 2019 World Water Week, Rammal (2019) noted that humanitarian sectors such as WASH have had to adapt in order to continue to meet the growing needs of those living through humanitarian crises. In a recent report, Sadoff et al. (2017) highlighted that, as emergencies deepen, WASH infrastructure falls into disrepair, complicating the WASH sector's ability to meet the short-term and long-term needs of those living in crisis. Mason et al. argue that:

> in such contexts, a lack of complementarity and collaboration between humanitarian and development WASH actors has heavy consequences, making it more costly to provide WASH services, reducing the effectiveness of targeting and sustainability, and ultimately increasing the vulnerability of poor people to disease and missed socio-economic opportunities. (Mason et al., 2017: 1)

Although these challenges are not unique to the WASH sector, there is a recognizable gap between the humanitarian and development sectors. Progress, however, is being made, with changes in the ways in which emergency funding streams are structured to better meet humanitarian priorities while moving towards long-term development goals. Through the case studies provided here, we aim to highlight examples of how organizations in humanitarian contexts have succeeded in building integrated WASH programming across the humanitarian–development divide.

The new way of working

The 2016 World Humanitarian Summit stated that collaboration across the humanitarian and development nexus is essential for an effective humanitarian response. Termed *New Way of Working* (OCHA, 2017), this push is the latest iteration of a much older debate that seeks to connect short-term humanitarian action with long-term development goals. However, changes of this magnitude will require significant collaboration across sectors, to 'remove the wedge that currently drives the two worlds apart – building on the strengths and capacities of existing organisations and sector structures from the ground up, rather than inventing new global initiatives from the top down' (Mason et al., 2017: 1). As we argued in a previous publication, 'this change will not only require innovation in how humanitarian and development WASH organisations collaborate but real recruitment, organisational, and systematic changes that will allow WASH programs to save more lives and build resilience in the future' (Sorensen and Snel, 2020: 278). In this publication, we highlight some positive progress towards WASH integration across the humanitarian and development nexus, while continuing to develop a vision for further change.

This recent focus on integration across the humanitarian and development nexus is nothing new. Still, it highlights the reality that, in the international development community, there has been a clear distinction between those working in the area of WASH from a humanitarian perspective – namely, focusing on short-term, emergency WASH issues – and those working on longer-term development needs. What is happening globally, especially in regions such as the Middle East, is the development of a more explicit range of WASH services that span three phases: humanitarian services, which typically cover the first six months; a transitional phase, often between six months to two years; and, finally, longer-term WASH after two years and beyond.

Within humanitarian settings, the scale, duration, and complexity of humanitarian crises are increasing due to rapid population growth (Lattimer and Swithern, 2017).Yet, over the last decade, there have been several systematic reviews that have concluded that WASH interventions in humanitarian crises yield essential health and social benefits for vulnerable affected populations (Brown et al., 2012; Bastable and Russell, 2013; Ramesh et al., 2015; Blanchet et al., 2017; Yates et al., 2017b; 2017a). However, the current evidence base supporting humanitarian WASH interventions is still relatively limited, with policy and practice often based on operational experience rather than independent evaluation. Also, research has been dominated by studies of household or point-of-use water treatment; there has been little research on community WASH interventions' health or social impacts or on the relative benefits of combined WASH interventions. Finally, evidence generation in humanitarian crises remains challenging and ad hoc (Lattimer and Swithern, 2017).

There is substantive literature focusing on emergency interventions moving towards transitional, longer-term development (VOICE and CONCORD, 2012; European Commission, 2014; Mason et al., 2017). However, this research provides limited information on what transitional WASH programming looks like as it moves from emergency responses to longer-term development (Ramesh et al., 2015; Bennett et al., 2016; Lloyd, 2017; Mason et al., 2017; World Bank et al., 2021).

To some extent, there have always been professional silos between emergency and development WASH, likely rooted in the early development of WASH in the 1970s, which focused on either immediate emergency needs or long-term WASH programmes (Mason and Mosello, 2016). However, in the realities of WASH today, there are far more shades of grey between these two sectors, thus calling into question the traditional silo approach. How can we intentionally focus on the three phases of WASH (humanitarian, transitional, and long-term) in a way that provides sustainable WASH services across the humanitarian and development spectrum?

Delivering sustainable WASH services

Fragile and extremely fragile contexts are a growing concern for the humanitarian sector. As crises grow in number and duration, predominantly in fragile contexts, the ability of international organizations to deliver sustainable WASH services diminishes. It is estimated that 'more than two billion people live in 58 fragile, including 15 extremely and conflict-affected contexts, and it is estimated by 2030 approximately 80 percent of the world's poor will live in such contexts' (German WASH Network, 2019: 2). The WASH sector is already facing significant funding gaps as humanitarian organizations try to meet current needs. Before the coronavirus (COVID-19) outbreak, only half of these 58 fragile and extremely fragile contexts were on track to meet Sustainable Development Goal (SDG) 6 for clean water and sanitation by 2030 (OECD, 2020: 32), and the COVID pandemic has already significantly impacted both the funding and the achievement of various SDGs. A research report conducted by Hutton and Varughese (2016) indicated that, although the WASH sector needs three times more funding to reach SDG 6, achieving clean water and sanitation for all was within reach. However with the ongoing global COVID pandemic, which has also increased further conflict, war, and economic disasters, we are further away from this SDG goal (Tobin, 2020).

With inadequate funding to meet the current need, organizations are often reduced to delivering short-term solutions that generate high long-term costs. Providing sustainable WASH services that reduce the vulnerability of those living in crisis 'demands that humanitarian and development organisations align from the start and consider the fragility and conflict dynamics in which interventions are taking place, to support interventions that are conflict-sensitive and establish WASH sector resilience' (UNICEF, 2019: 2).

Although the bulk of this book focuses on bridging the humanitarian–development gap, it is essential to note that another crucial division is between the humanitarian and development silos and the governments affected by humanitarian crises. This is often referred to as the triple nexus between the humanitarian, development, and peace sectors. Robust WASH services that allow humanitarian interventions to bridge the development and peace nexus begin with good governance. Naylor and Gordon (2020) argue that, in order to accelerate this process, sanitation needs to be redefined as an 'essential public good', allowing the benefits of WASH services to reach all people in society, not just the most affluent. A joint report on sanitation, developed by the United Nations Children's Fund (UNICEF) and the World Health Organization (WHO), highlights five key accelerators that would help governments jump-start effective sanitation services: good governance, smart public finance, capacity building, reliable data, and innovation (UNICEF and WHO, 2020: 12–13):

- Good governance is essential as a leadership structure for effective coordination between funders, humanitarian responders, and development organizations. Policymaking and strong regulations set the stage for long-term WASH success and require collaboration and a shared vision across the triple nexus; they are also vital to effective localization.
- Smart public finance facilitates coordination and cooperation between humanitarian, development, and government organizations and lays a foundation for safe WASH services. Strong government policy, with robust regulations around WASH, is critical in attracting private sector investment into damaged or non-existent WASH infrastructure. Mobilizing funding streams from multiple sources beyond international aid is vital to the long-term sustainability of WASH programmes and allows governments

and humanitarian responders to quickly and sustainably reach the most vulnerable populations.

- Capacity building in the WASH sector requires system changes to assist organizations and to facilitate integration across all humanitarian and development departments. WASH programming is becoming intersectoral. Capacity will have to grow and new skills developed if governments are to bring together the range of public and private partners necessary to meet the ambitious SDGs.
- Reliable data is everything. It leads to better and faster decision making and is essential to increasing impact for the most marginalized populations. Accountability comes from timely, high-quality data and is necessary for progress to be made.
- Finally, innovation is vital. New approaches are needed to meet emerging challenges such as urbanization, population growth, and climate change, all of which will increase the costs of humanitarian WASH interventions in an already cash-strapped sector. As we discuss in this book, new ways of looking at the WASH sector are required if we are to get anywhere close to meeting the SDGs in 2030.

As mentioned above, reliable data is essential for governments to accelerate WASH initiatives. It is also of vital importance in the humanitarian sector. There is a severe lack of reliable research supporting WASH programming in humanitarian contexts. D'Mello-Guyett et al. highlight this gap, arguing:

> This paucity of evidence is reflected in guideline recommendations for humanitarian WASH programmes, such as the Sphere standards, which are often not supported by rigorous, published evidence. Although many response agencies routinely conduct programme evaluations, these are often not rigorous nor published; thereby limiting the uptake of findings. While this issue is common across the humanitarian sector, a systematic review of all public health interventions in humanitarian crises published in 2017, found that WASH interventions were supported by far fewer studies ($n = 6$) than other areas of public health. (D'Mello-Guyett et al., 2018: 1)

Standard indicators (see Annex 1) used by humanitarian WASH programmes, development organizations, and government institutions will strengthen the integration and transition of WASH programming across the humanitarian, development, and peace nexus.

The Global WASH Cluster recently finalized the 2020–25 road map around a vision that, 'by 2025, the WASH sector will have the capacity and resources to deliver in emergencies at scale, anywhere and any time' (Global WASH Cluster, 2019: 5). The road map highlights a path forward by emphasizing the three axes required to improve operational methods and three prerequisite pillars for functional capacity in the humanitarian WASH sector (see Figure 1.1).

Vision

By 2025, the WASH sector will have
the capacity and resources to deliver in
emergencies at scale, anywhere and any time

**IMPROVED OPERATING METHODS
IN THE HUMANITARIAN WASH SECTOR**

Axis 1

The humanitarian WASH response is life-saving and driven by public and environmental health outcomes.

Axis 2

The humanitarian WASH response consistently meets agreed accountability and the highest quality standards.

Axis 3

The humanitarian WASH response is predictable and results in sustainable impacts rooted in preparedness and resilience.

Strategic initiatives (axes)
• protocols and systems development • interlinkages with other sectors • knowledge management • thematic capacity-building • quality assurance and accountability systems • mainstreaming of safe programming and CCI • operational toolkits development • global monitoring system set up • resilient, preparedness and risk priorities • engagement of development stakeholders

**PREREQUISITE PILLARS FOR A FUNCTIONAL CAPACITY
IN THE HUMANITARIAN WASH SECTOR**

**Pillar 1
Capacity**

The humanitarian WASH response has the right systems, at the right place, at the right time

**Pillar 2
Coordination and partnership**

The humanitarian WASH response is sustained by leadership and strategic partnerships

**Pillar 3
Financing**

The humanitarian WASH response is supported by innovative, flexible and predictable funding

Strategic initiatives (pillars)
• structural capacity-building (international, local actors, service providers) • harmonized, system-wide approach • coordination mechanisms and information management systems • strategic and operational partnerships • sector-financing and investments • dedicated global fund

Figure 1.1 The three axes and three pillars of WASH
Source: Global WASH Cluster (2019: 5). Reproduced with permission from UNICEF.

The three axes present a clear vision of what WASH is and what it can accomplish, while the three pillars set a basis for how humanitarian WASH can achieve that vision. This development creates the necessary foundation for effective humanitarian WASH responses in the future; this is essential to the effective integration of humanitarian WASH with development and peace priorities.

The sustainable WASH delivery model

Sustainable WASH delivery requires strong and competent national and local government systems to be in place. Creating WASH programmes that align across the humanitarian and development nexus produces a sound, sustainable WASH model as part of the WASH systems approach. This model was developed historically by WEDC and further elaborated by others, including the WASH Alliance International, and reflects on five critical aspects of sustainable WASH: financial, institutional, environmental, technological, and social. It is referred to as the FIETS sustainability approach (WASH Alliance International, n.d.).

- Financial sustainability refers to using locally procured resources such as community fees, for example through a community maintenance model, to provide continuous WASH products and services.
- Institutional sustainability relies on local and national policies, institutions, and stakeholders to provide and manage WASH services through clear expectations and adequate funding, personnel, and resources.
- Environmental sustainability ensures that local and national water sources are protected and maintained through integrated programming and resource management.
- Technological sustainability is achieved when local capabilities are sufficient to maintain, repair, and upgrade WASH infrastructure and maintain continuous and safe WASH services.
- Social sustainability provides adequate WASH services in a socially acceptable way while protecting stakeholders' dignity (WASH Alliance International, n.d.).

Figure 1.2 illustrates how sustainable WASH requires the integration of these five key areas.

Currently, a joint operational framework is being developed by the Global WASH Cluster with the German WASH Network; this aligns Sanitation for All as well as the IRC building blocks towards sustainable WASH services (SWA, 2020a). For this publication we have focused on the basic FIETS model which encompasses these building blocks.

WASH practitioners can further reflect on the sustainable WASH model in line with the three WASH phases: humanitarian, transitional, and longer-term WASH programming. Figure 1.3 shows several key characteristics in each stage and is adapted from Mason et al. (2017) and Harvey et al. (2020). This list is not exclusive but instead provides an overview of the distinctions between the subsectors.

Finally, our discussion in Chapter 2 looks at current norms in the humanitarian and development sectors, and at the realities of each subsector of the sustainable WASH delivery model, with a particular focus on WASH financing.

Figure 1.2 The FIETS sustainability approach

Source: Snel (2018). Reproduced with permission from World Vision.

Chapter 3 presents several case studies that highlight key points that WASH practitioners should keep in mind as they consider WASH programme design in current and future humanitarian crises. These case studies are drawn from various Save the Children[4] and World Vision International[5] programmes and highlight how humanitarian organizations are beginning to bridge the humanitarian–development divide. They are not perfect examples but they do illustrate themes linking the sustainable WASH model and integrated WASH programming across the humanitarian and development nexus. Chapter 4 discusses the critical role non-household settings play in developing an integrated and sustainable approach to humanitarian WASH responses. We argue that these already existing institutional settings can further play a fundamentally decisive role in integrating emergency WASH interventions with other critical sectors and in filling gaps and decreasing the risks faced by vulnerable populations. Finally, in Chapter 5, we look at the future of emergency WASH, what future WASH professionals will look like, and what they will need to know to succeed in the challenges humanitarian environments will face in the future.

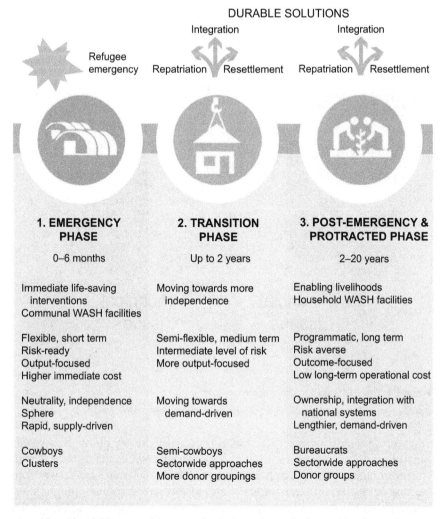

Figure 1.3 Characteristics of the WASH nexus
Source: Snel (2018), adapted from Mason et al. (2017) and Harvey et al. (2020).
Reproduced with permission from World Vision.

Notes

1. Our survey was conducted in May and June 2020 and comprised eight open-ended questions. It was sent to approximately 45 WASH professionals, from which we received 13 detailed responses representing 10 major organizations.
2. We conducted 14 interviews with a range of WASH professionals between June 2020 and February 2021. These comprised three open-ended questions:

'What do you believe is one of the key successes in starting to build the bridge between the humanitarian and development divide linked to WASH?'; 'What do you believe is one of the key challenges (e.g. financial, institutional, political, environmental) in starting to build the bridge between the humanitarian and development divide linked to WASH?'; and 'What is the key future development that you see emerging in the WASH sector in the coming 10–15 years?'

3. The 'Triple Nexus in WASH' meeting took place on 11–12 February 2021 and was organized by the German WASH network in collaboration with the Global WASH Cluster, Sanitation and Water for All (SWA), UNICEF, and German Humanitarian Assistance.

4. Although both authors have worked with Save the Children US in the past, and at the time this book was written one author was currently working with Save the Children US, the views and opinions expressed here are those of the authors and do not necessarily reflect the official policy or position of any agency.

5. Although one of the authors has worked with World Vision International in the past, the views and opinions expressed here are those of the authors and do not necessarily reflect the official policy or position of any agency.

CHAPTER 2
Considerations around WASH and the nexus

Achieving humanitarian outcomes that lead towards long-term goals is essential to building resilience in the future. This resilience is built through collaboration – and, above all, trust – highlighting the need for governments, organizations, and communities to work together to build humanitarian and development outcomes in fragile contexts. In UNICEF's *Strategy for Water, Sanitation and Hygiene 2016–2030*, it is stated that:

> Response to humanitarian crises must be a continuum between rapid response and longer-term solutions that build resilience of communities and sector systems to endure shocks and crisis. An investment during times of stability can effectively mitigate negative impacts during crisis and similarly, to the extent possible, use of development systems and stakeholders can contribute to long-term goals. (UNICEF, 2016: 15)

At the beginning of 2020, UNHCR, the UN Refugee Agency, and UNICEF developed a two-year 'Blueprint for Joint Action'. The blueprint is a commitment to accelerate joint efforts under a transformational agenda in line with the *Global Compact on Refugees* (2018). It applies across the humanitarian–development nexus to ensure that no refugee, vulnerable host community, or child is left behind. The initial phase of this new partnership focuses on three sectors – education, WASH, and child protection – across 11 countries.[1] This work is still ongoing, with different levels of success, as cited by one of the interviewees.

Bridging the WASH humanitarian–development nexus is a complicated commitment. However, rather than underscoring the complexity in the steps ahead, we focus here on some of the key WASH elements from financial, political, institutional, social, and environmental perspectives, highlighting the broader context that needs to be considered when bridging the WASH humanitarian and development spectrum. Integration across these five key considerations is vital in creating the coordination necessary to reduce the impact of future emergencies. Portions of this chapter are based on a paper originally published in *Waterlines* in October 2020 (Sorensen and Snel, 2020). Here, we connect those arguments with further conversations we have had with other WASH professionals.

WASH financing

Funding within the WASH sector is one of the most significant barriers and greatest opportunities for integrated programming. Although WASH funding has increased over the last few years, this growth is insufficient to meet current and growing needs. This financial discrepancy shows the extent to which the humanitarian and development sectors remain in silos; both sectors need further adaptation to meet future circumstances (Fanning and Fullwood-Thomas, 2019). There is no significant difference between the humanitarian and the development response for those who live in acute crisis conditions, as both are about survival and rebuilding lives.

In 2016, the Humanitarian World Summit officially launched the 'Grand Bargain' (IASC, n.d.) as part of the agenda for humanity. This meeting brought together the largest aid organizations and donors and created a collective promise to provide 25 per cent of global humanitarian funding to local and national responders by 2020. This was achieved through a commitment to more multi-year funding streams that focus on providing predictability in the humanitarian response. The theory that led to the Grand Bargain was that, 'if donors and agencies each make changes, aid delivery will become more efficient, freeing up human and financial resources for the direct benefit of affected populations' (ICVA, 2017: 3). This agreement was initially conceived in recognition of the growing humanitarian financing gap that was outlined in a high-level UN report in 2016 (United Nations, 2016). To date, however, there has been disagreement about whether this has taken place in alignment with further decentralization and localization agendas (Brabant and Patel, 2018).

Although humanitarian investment has seen a considerable increase since 2014, that increase has not been sufficient to meet current humanitarian needs, especially within the WASH sector. As crises worldwide grow in number and length, funding deficits become a critical concern, and WASH is one of the consistently underfunded sectors. On average, only about 45 per cent of WASH funding requirements are met, despite their importance (Grünewald et al., 2019). This gap puts significant pressure on humanitarian and development WASH practitioners to consider alternative funding streams so that they can continue to meet the needs of the people they seek to help. Acknowledging these considerable funding gaps, Hutton argued that universal access to adequate water and sanitation should be the target for WASH practitioners, but 'caution[ed] that WASH targets should be realistic – in terms of how fast it is likely WASH services can be scaled up with the available financing and local implementation capacities' (Hutton, 2015: 1) within targeted countries.

Another critical question that needs to be asked relates to the mechanisms through which key implementing donors such as UNICEF and UNHCR receive their funding. In UNICEF's case, funding comes from the voluntary contributions of governments, intergovernmental organizations, foundations, the private sector, and individuals. UNICEF WASH departments can establish new funding resources. In UNHCR, they rely almost entirely on voluntary contributions from governments and the UN, pooled funding mechanisms, intergovernmental institutions, and the private sector. The UNHCR WASH department cannot initiate funding resources or work with other partners to bring in further funding for WASH.

There will be more focus now than ever before on public–private partnerships,[2] as shown in various publications and case studies. A recent example of a public–private WASH partnership can be found in Cox's Bazaar, Bangladesh; this is a sound financial partnership between key donors, government, and private sector actors (World Bank, 2020). However, it should be kept in mind that this development has taken place since the start of the Rohingya refugee crisis at the end of 2016.

Weak financial structures interweaved with institutional weakness continue to play a vital role. For example, in the context of a Somali case study, Jama and Mourad argue that:

> Institutions involved in the water sector in Puntland are not well organized. Roles and responsibilities were unclear, and different governmental institutions criticized each other for deliberately taking over others' responsibilities, leading to poor and over-priced domestic water quality. (Jama and Mourad, 2019)

Their conclusion was that financial as well as institutional reforms are needed 'in the water sector in order to achieve SDG 6 (Target One) and to ensure safe drinking water in Puntland by 2030' (Jama and Mourad, 2019). Another case study in Ethiopia relating to sanitation coverage reflects the importance of collaboration across sectors through the use of public–private partnerships. This case highlights the possibilities of public–private partnerships but states that 'the potential of collaboration for stimulating market growth is not sufficiently realized to meet sanitation-related SDG targets' (Johansson and Debrework, 2017: 1). However, further public–private collaboration can lead to sustainable development, production, and distribution through commercially viable and accountable business models that improve SDG outcomes.

The recent COVID-19 pandemic and the 2014–15 Ebola outbreak have strengthened the argument for further integration within the humanitarian silo. Integration could be vital to stabilizing health, nutrition, and WASH funding. It allows humanitarian responders to take advantage of their unique access to beneficiaries to impact a broad array of individuals with programming from multiple sectors. When this book was written, the COVID-19 outbreak was continuing to spread, with a new and stronger mutated version circling the globe. As such, it is anticipated that, over the next few years, funding for health-related programming is likely to see a substantial increase, and this is only going to exacerbate funding inequality. A focus on integration will allow WASH programming to continue to play its crucial part in the COVID-19 response and in future humanitarian crises. Integrating WASH with health, nutrition, and other sectors will allow WASH practitioners to shift their focus from maintaining their portion of the humanitarian funding pie to expanding into new, innovative financing streams. This requires a perspective shift on the part of funders, from donors all the way down to the WASH professionals themselves, in terms of how to view funding in, say, health, nutrition, or education through an integration lens and as an opportunity to meet WASH outcomes as well.

Although funding through WASH and Cash is not a new phenomenon, as reflected in the work done by the Overseas Development Institute (ODI, 2015; Mason and Mosello, 2016), including in collaboration with Save the Children UK (Le Seve and Mason, 2019), this is one area that has started to play a more significant role, alongside WASH integration developments.

Although integrating WASH with health and nutrition is a vital step in stabilizing funding streams, integration alone is not enough to overcome the consequences of underfunding. To meet both the WASH requirements of future governments and organizations and growing water needs, humanitarian and development workers will have to innovate. Fonseca and Pories indicate that taxes, tariffs, and external transfers are currently the only three WASH funding sources available to developing countries. However, they highlight that 'the combination of these funding sources is not sufficient to address the need for water and sanitation services in developing countries' (Fonseca and Pories, 2017: 5).

In 2010, the Organisation for Economic Co-operation and Development (OECD) set out these three 'T's of WASH service financing: tariffs, taxes, and transfers. In their recent publication, however, Danert and Hutton point out that:

> The 2010 OECD publication states that while there are hundreds of financiers in water and sanitation that all finance originates from three main sources, those being donors (=transfers), public funds from the government (=taxes) and what customers pay out of their pocket for their services (=tariffs). The private sector is not explicitly included but rather incorporated in the tariffs paid by customers, if there is full cost recovery from the user or partially paid by taxes or transfers in the case of public–private partnerships. (Danert and Hutton, 2020: 1)

Keeping this observation in mind, Danert and Hutton further argue that using 'the three "T"s financing source framework (taxes, tariffs and transfers) leads us to ignore key costs to the customer, especially the poor customer, of accessing an adequate level of the water, sanitation and hygiene (WASH) service' (Danert and Hutton, 2020: 1). Danert and Hutton (2020) go on to propose adding household investment to the three 'T's to better capture household-level interaction with WASH services.[3] With the current COVID-19 outbreak as a backdrop, there is no better opportunity to test and redefine new funding sources, to remind new and existing funders about the integrated role WASH plays in health responses, and to mobilize them behind additional WASH strategies.

Multi-year funding for humanitarian responses is an often discussed solution to this issue. This change would factor in the protracted nature of most humanitarian crises and allow for better alignment of humanitarian and development actors. The vast majority of humanitarian appeals are for short periods – many are for less than a year in length – but they are then often extended for five or more years. Grünewald et al. argue that '[t]his short-term approach is detrimental to resilience efforts during protracted crises, as it leads to insufficient timeframes to either lessen the impacts of disasters or to strengthen the capacity for an effective humanitarian response should a disaster overwhelm prevention measures' (2019: 39). They go on to say: 'Multi-year planning and appeals are critical to ensure that the preparedness and prevention measures necessary for a resilient WASH sector are put in place' (Grünewald et al., 2019: 39). These shifts would allow humanitarian aid programmes to plan for integration and would facilitate a broader, more efficient dissemination of life-saving interventions in crisis areas. However, achieving this integration requires short-term funding structures to become more flexible, allowing their use on system-strengthening programmes with long-term aims in mind, as reflected in the SWA and IRC building blocks (Huston and Moriarty, 2018; SWA, 2020b).

Although multi-year funding in the humanitarian sector may lead to some level of stabilization of WASH funding, the real opportunity for funding growth in the future will likely be found in alternative funding sources, most notably through blended financing. Blended financing is the use of both public and private financing with a development mandate (including philanthropists' money) to attract or leverage further public and private commercial money (requiring a return on investment) to finance the development programme. The Global WASH Cluster's road map for 2020–25 seeks the 'use of emerging models or blended approaches that strategically combine and optimize aid, public and private funds' (Global WASH Cluster, 2019: 16). However, the most substantial barrier to private financing is the risk incurred by the private sector. There is a tremendous opportunity for outbreak response funding to be connected to preventative integrated WASH programming as a means of building incentives for further investment in unstable crises. This is why Fonseca and Pories argue that it is essential for governments to increase investments in water and sanitation systems, which 'would give private financial institutions more confidence to invest in these countries and utilities' (Fonseca and Pories, 2017: 9). With COVID-19, there is a tremendous opportunity for outbreak response funding to be connected to preventative integrated WASH programming as a means of building these incentives for further investment.

Blended financing requires careful planning to get the balance right. Still, if done correctly, it can free up public resources and aid governments in building longer-lasting, more stable WASH systems. As Fonseca and Pories also highlight, blended financing uses 'public taxes, development grants and concessional loans to mobilize private capital flows to emerging and frontier markets – [it] can leverage additional funds for the sector and reduce borrowing costs as compared to a fully commercial arrangement' (Fonseca and Pories, 2017: 15). De Albuquerque argued in a Devex interview that the first part of this balance will be found in the way in which 'governments and their partners work with the financing sources they already have but are underutilized: domestic water tariffs, taxes, and micro and macro loans' (Devex Editor, 2020). De Albuquerque, currently leading Sanitation and Water for All (SWA), argues that, by using existing resources more efficiently and securing private sector funding, governments and development firms would be able to focus their resources on tackling the 'non-sexy, invisible issues such as independent regulation, policies, and capacity building' with fewer high-interest loans (Devex Editor, 2020).

In line with ongoing external pressures around climate change, the most recent SWA report on the 2020 Finance Ministers' Meetings further reflects, for example, that '[g]reen financing, green bonds, social impact bonds and other innovative financing mechanisms can secure additional funding that support [sic] both the delivery of better services, as well as long-term climate goals (SWA, 2020b). As concerns about the growing challenge of climate change intensify, new thinking around funding structures and future humanitarian and development responses is emerging. Viewed in this light, a focus on the environmental nexus could be most timely.

The COVID-19 outbreak makes a perfect case for further development in WASH sector funding, especially in alignment with the health and nutrition sector. The multisectoral nature of WASH makes it the key funding basis of a coordinated response to any outbreak. Resilience to future outbreaks will require a stronger worldwide WASH foundation to build upon, especially in developing countries where WASH programmes are currently severely underfunded. Ideally, this multi-country, multi-sector requirement will be met through renewed and expanded WASH funding that extends across the humanitarian–development divide. At the time of writing this book, the Global WASH Cluster, as cited earlier, was in the process of strengthening the alignment of its humanitarian WASH work through the development of a joint operational framework to reflect the interconnections across organizations and sectors.

WASH political and institutional backing

As a means of bridging the humanitarian–development divide, organizations at the global level such as the World Bank, UNHCR, UNICEF, and INGOs are starting to show serious commitment to this discussion. In the *Strategy for Water, Sanitation and Hygiene 2016–2030*, UNICEF made a commitment that it:

> will encourage greater integration of humanitarian and development WASH programmes to improve both the effectiveness of humanitarian responses and the long-term sustainability of national WASH systems and of community resilience capacity. Using its expertise and leadership roles in both the humanitarian and development spheres, UNICEF will promote strengthened and more holistic sector coordination mechanisms. UNICEF will also ensure that emergency preparedness and prevention are standard components within national sector planning instruments. (UNICEF, 2016: 15)

UNICEF has reiterated this commitment to bridging the humanitarian–development divide in its most recent annual report (UNICEF, 2019) by acknowledging the need for better understanding and for the development of new ways of linking these two sectors. This is also evident with the new 'Blueprint for joint action' between UNHCR and UNICEF (2020). However, as cited earlier, this blueprint is still very much a work in progress and has struggled to gain traction.

As this book was being developed, a few key political and institutional events took place at the global level that ignited further discussion around the humanitarian and development nexus. One of the most recent events was the 'Building Resilient WASH Systems in Fragile States' workshop (December 2019 and February 2021) organized by the German WASH Network and linked to key collaborative partners such as UNICEF, SWA, the Global WASH Cluster, the International Committee of the Red Cross (ICRC), and the German Humanitarian Assistance, as mentioned earlier.[4] As the workshop report from 2019 acknowledges, 'Although the WASH sector as a whole is not very advanced in building bridges between the humanitarian and development realms, there are currently many initiatives with good momentum' (German WASH Network, 2019: 3). Recently, events like this have focused far more on perspectives of collaboration, capacity development, and finance rather than on specific examples of how these can be achieved. This situation emphasizes the need for publications like this one, which provide a stronger foundation of WASH-related case studies and practical research on realities from the field. This vital underpinning acknowledges the need for collaboration, capacity development, and financial reform in the WASH sector while providing concrete examples of innovation, demonstrating how organizations are bridging the WASH humanitarian–development divide.

However, one cannot underestimate the fact that a political realm in which refugee settings are always considered 'temporary' continues to pose serious political issues for the host country. Constructing structural infrastructure is hard work. As one key UNHCR staff member stated in an interview:

> We are in the blind if this [refugee settlement] will be a temporary situation or one that will be there for the next 5, 10, 15 or more years. [Often] UNHCR is left with the [empty] bag while all the other [humanitarian] NGOs leave … In other words, the humanitarian is left between a rock and a hard place.[5]

Global framework developments around the WASH nexus

The two recent workshops organized by the German WASH Network with key partners mentioned above brought together several key organizations to discuss the role of WASH systems within the humanitarian and development sector. A critical thematic focus was on building a more holistic understanding of how to implement WASH systems in humanitarian and development settings and identifying and dismantling barriers that block the realization of inclusive, sustainable, and universal access to WASH.

Consequently, as we were finalizing this publication, SWA[6] started to focus on developing a framework for system strengthening. This included four 'collaborative behaviours', defining how partners can best work together to deliver the building blocks for stronger WASH systems (Huston and Moriarty, 2018; SWA, 2020b). The SWA framework is linked to the 'mutual account-ability mechanism', which empowers partners to hold each other accountable for progress towards the SDGs. It provides a platform to break down collab-orative efforts into SMART actions and it reinforces country-level multi-stakeholder planning and review processes. The overarching Sanitation and Water for All (SWA) building blocks guide the whole process (SWA, 2020b). This reformulation of the SWA strategy provides a window of opportunity to harmonize SWA and Global WASH Cluster frameworks.

As discussed in Chapter 1, the Global WASH Cluster's road map focuses on three strategic axes and pillars. The pillars include a focus on capacity, coordination and partnership, and financing (Global WASH Cluster, 2019: 5). In an interview, Monica Ramos, the new Global WASH Cluster lead, noted that siloed responses used to be the norm but that now there is a greater focus on WASH service delivery across the humanitarian–development divide. As such, there is now a strong memorandum of understanding (MOU) being signed between SWA and the Global WASH Cluster, and they are starting to see successful results from these changes.[7] More stakeholders from the humanitarian and development WASH sectors are coming together from the start, especially in key meetings such as the triple WASH nexus meeting.[8] In other words, there is a strategy emerging for how bilateral donors will need to work more closely together, given existing and increasing crises in fragile contexts.

Alongside this development, Dominick de Waal from the World Bank noted in an interview that, as we move forward in bridging the humanitarian–development divide, coordination via global, regional, and national WASH platforms will continue to be fundamental.[9] This will also require government ownership, which means that the government will be in the driver's seat and orchestrate the division of labour. This, as he noted, will need institutional reconfigurations. For example, water authorities might receive long-term development funding and short-term emergency funding for the same water system, requiring entirely different management and reporting and leading to potentially conflicting outcomes. In another interview, the former head of the WASH department at UNHCR, Murray Burt, stated: 'There is a need for flexible funding in order to make influential changes.'[10] This, according to him, entails understanding funding from both the humanitarian and the development side. It also requires a focus on increased, intentional funding flexibility resulting from fast-track grants in emergency situations, leading to programming that crosses the humanitarian–development divide. In other words, further alignment over time at the global, regional, and national level is essential for sustainable WASH delivery across the humanitarian–development divide.

Development of the nexus

Integration across the humanitarian and development nexus can be vital to successfully navigate the complex crises of the future – specifically, protracted emergencies, disease outbreaks, climate change, and food insecurity. DuBois argues that a new humanitarian mindset is needed to address these problems, one that 'conceives of short-term action within a long-term vision of needs; pays attention to the long-term consequences of humanitarian approaches on development or peace; and exchanges analysis and views organically across multi-sector teams' (DuBois, 2020). In an interview, Michael Talhami from ICRC stated that the 'seek to do no harm' approach is also important 'in our longer-term response', referring to one of the most significant publications to date on protracted crises and why conflict management is so important (ICRC, 2020).[11]

Social development with a new mindset

The development of this new mindset will require the retraining of humanitarian and development practitioners and significant changes in the structure of funding appeals as well as in implementors' organizational structures. Furthermore, for these structures to succeed, Fanning and Fullwood-Thomas explain that:

> This will require consensus-building, brokering and building new partnerships; navigating and communicating complex ideas; using systems thinking; facilitating open dialogues; and co-creating ideas. Investment is needed to develop joint tools, analysis and language, and to ensure that the views of people affected by crises are integrated at every step, and local leadership comes to the fore. All of this will require flexible funding instruments and changes in programme management structures. (Fanning and Fullwood-Thomas, 2019: 5)

In principle, integration across the nexus not only facilitates better alignment between humanitarian and development interventions tailored to the immediate realities of people in crisis; it also allows aid workers responding to disease outbreaks, climate change, food insecurity, and other protracted crises to tie life-saving interventions into the long-term needs and goals of those they serve. DuBois (2016) articulated further that 'the urgency of food, water, healthcare or shelter needs in Syria or eastern DRC displaces but does not diminish the longer-term hopes and aspirations of people in terms of wanting economic progress, a functioning healthcare system or political empowerment'. It is also here that WASH could play a further vital role in non-household settings such as schools, healthcare facilities, refugee and IDP (internally displaced persons) camps, and other locations. To this end, saving lives during a crisis must be explicitly connected to the long-term expectations and aspirations of the people being served.

Environmental sustainability

As noted earlier, environmental sustainability implies placing WASH interventions in the broader context of the natural environment and implementing the integrated and sustainable management of water and waste (water) flows and resources. WASH interventions connect to and affect the natural environment and hence people's livelihoods. Environmental sustainability in WASH entails deep reflection on the ways in which WASH programming impacts landscape, water systems, flows, and local community needs. This requires a focus on the 3R approach: namely, recharge, retention, and reuse of water resources, or, in the context of waste, reduce, reuse, and recycle. We must protect and maintain the natural resources and services upon which communities rely through WASH programme design aimed at low-cost, low-maintenance, environmentally friendly technologies such as solar energy and through a focus on ecosystem services approaches.

With increasing population growth and urbanization, water competition and scarcity will be two of the most significant issues WASH professionals face in the future (Mason and Mosello, 2016). The humanitarian WASH sector will have to pivot as climate change responses become an increasing part of humanitarian and development programming; this will also necessitate integration with other sectors such as health, nutrition, and agriculture. This is further complicated by the increase in the number and duration of crises facing the world. As cited in a 2019 Global WASH Cluster report, 'the WASH sector currently does not have the resources to cope with multiple level 2 or 3 disasters taking place at the same time in different parts of the world, and lasting a relatively long time' (Grünewald et al., 2019: 10).

Notes

1. The 11 countries are Bangladesh, Cameroon, Ecuador, Ethiopia, Honduras, Indonesia, Iraq, Kenya, Lebanon, Libya, and Rwanda.
2. A public–private partnership (PPP) can be defined as 'a long-term contract between a private party and government entity, for providing a public asset or service, in which the private party bears significant risk and management responsibility, and remuneration is linked to performance' (see 'PPP reference guide' at <https://pppknowledgelab.org/guide/sections/3-what-is-a-ppp-defining-public-private-partnership>).
3. Based on survey responses by 25 national governments in 2016–17, the *Global Analysis and Assessment of Sanitation and Drinking-Water (GLAAS)* reports that an estimated 66 per cent of US$43 billion annual WASH expenditure (i.e. US$28 billion) comes from household contributions (WHO, 2017).

4. Following a working meeting on WASH systems in fragile contexts at ODI in 2018, an informal group of INGOs was formed. This group held a workshop on the topic during the 'All Systems Go!' symposium in the Hague in March 2019 and is now writing a working paper on the application of WASH systems approaches in fragile contexts.
5. Interview conducted by Mariëlle Snel, 23 February 2021.
6. SWA is a global partnership committed to achieving universal access to clean drinking water and adequate sanitation (see <https://www.globalwaters.org/globalprograms/sanitation-and-water-all>).
7. Interview conducted by Mariëlle Snel, 4 November 2020.
8. The triple WASH nexus (humanitarian, development, peace) meeting was organized by the German WASH Network in collaboration with the Global WASH Cluster, UNICEF, and SWA. It took place on 11–12 February 2021. At the time this book was being submitted, the workshop report was yet to be published.
9. Interview conducted by Mariëlle Snel and Nikolas Sorensen, 18 June 2020.
10. Interview conducted by Mariëlle Snel and Nikolas Sorensen, 19 June 2020.
11. Interview conducted by Mariëlle Snel, 1 December 2020.

CHAPTER 3
Country case studies from the field

These case studies from WASH programmes in Nigeria, Afghanistan, Jordan, and Yemen are not perfect examples where the humanitarian–development nexus is bridged wonderfully, but they show recent programmes that grapple with the real issues around sustainable WASH. They are intended to add depth and practicality to the ongoing conversation surrounding the humanitarian and development nexus. Ideas and themes can be picked out from them, not necessarily as best practice, but rather to promote thinking and discussion. The case studies are drawn from Save the Children and World Vision International programmes and were collected with the help of programme managers working in Africa, Asia, and the Middle East (the Myanmar case study is featured in Chapter 4). Each case study starts with an introduction followed by interventions. Several of the case studies also highlight relevant challenges to success.

The case studies are followed by a section highlighting some further initiatives run by World Vision International from 2016 to 2018 (Snel, 2018) and by the International Water and Sanitation Centre (IRC) in 2013–15 (Snel and Verhoeven, 2016). We then offer our own reflections on the humanitarian and development nexus, drawing on insights from these case studies and the sustainable WASH model discussed in Chapter 2.

Box 3.1 Nigeria: integrated WASH programming

Save the Children
Acknowledgement: Umar Bishara

Introduction

The violent conflict between the Nigerian Security Forces and non-state armed groups has been ongoing since 2009. This decade-long conflict has seen more than 27,000 people killed, more than 4,000 people have been abducted, and 1.8 million people are currently displaced (OCHA, 2020b).

The Nigerian government declared a state of emergency in Borno, Adamawa, and Yobe states in May 2013 as clashes between the government and warring groups escalated. The conflict has led to mass displacement and restricted movement due to the region's violence and insecurity. Those impacted have seen a massive disruption to livelihoods, leading to food shortages and a lack of other essential resources. Furthermore, the conflict has destroyed infrastructure and hindered access to basic services, including education and primary healthcare. Moving forward, these three states will continue to experience population displacement and loss of life, with a huge impact on social and economic systems. The security and economic crisis will continue to exacerbate food insecurity, weaken the provision of health and nutrition services, and erode children's and their families' educational welfare.

(Continued)

Box 3.1 Continued

Intervention: integrated programming

Save the Children established operations in Borno and Yobe states in 2016, working to implement programmes related to their three breakthroughs for children: to ensure that children survive, learn, and are protected. With these three overarching goals, individual projects can focus on humanitarianism, on development, or on integrating the two. Child protection, education, nutrition, food security, livelihoods, and WASH activities all complement each other during a response. Save the Children uses integrated programming by training WASH staff, fieldworkers, and volunteers to connect WASH programming with Save the Children priorities for child protection, education, nutrition, food security, and livelihoods.

The WASH needs in north-east Nigeria remain very high, especially for children. There has been a significant increase in morbidity, increased spread of water-borne diseases such as cholera, and a lack of sanitation facilities and basic hygiene knowledge among IDPs and host community members.

Instead of running an individual WASH programme in Nigeria, WASH programming is integrated, thus providing a minimum WASH package in every possible intervention. In this way, beneficiaries receive holistic service coverage aimed at meeting their basic needs.

An important aspect of Save the Children's ability to work in an integrated manner has been strengthening evidence-based decision making. This has enabled the organization to establish trust with humanitarian donors and to introduce resilience activities into humanitarian programming. This has resulted in opportunities for programming across the humanitarian–development nexus, where evidence indicates that this would be beneficial. As the crisis continues, it has become vital for the humanitarian response to shift towards development. Although conflict continues in some regions of Nigeria, making it impossible to implement development priorities, it has become essential, where possible, to implement humanitarian responses with direct links to long-term development goals.

To address WASH needs in Nigeria across the humanitarian–development divide, Save the Children is currently running multiple projects to meet the short-term and long-term needs of beneficiaries. For example, a Food for Peace project aims to meet IDPs' and other vulnerable groups' short-term humanitarian WASH needs. This is connected with EU-funded projects that rehabilitate and renovate WASH facilities in schools and communities. Rehabilitating permanent WASH facilities encourages IDPs to return home when safe, building future resilience and allowing beneficiaries to focus on rebuilding their lives. Furthermore, these rehabilitated WASH facilities in non-household and community locations have employed people with disabilities to maintain and clean them. These types of initiative reduce the spread of disease and infection by providing clean WASH facilities and connect WASH programming to the community's social needs by providing opportunities for often overlooked individuals.

Box 3.2 Afghanistan: combined humanitarian, development, and disaster risk reduction projects

World Vision
Acknowledgement: Rosanna Keam

Introduction

The 2018 drought in Afghanistan, the worst seen in over a decade, displaced an estimated 298,000 people, particularly those living in Badghis and Herat provinces, in the search for water. Afghanistan is struggling to cope with the long-term consequences of climate

(Continued)

Box 3.2 Continued

change, the mismanagement of water resources, and four decades of conflict that have seriously impacted its water infrastructure. The drought, which acutely affected western Afghanistan, highlights how weak policy in an already fragile environment compounds the hardships faced by already marginalized populations in the area.

The region's primary water source is rainfall, which infiltrates groundwater systems that feed karezes, springs, and wells. Karezes are underground irrigation tunnels bored horizontally into rock slopes, an ancient water supply system found throughout Afghanistan. They rely on rain and snowfall, which slowly infiltrate the groundwater systems and replenish them. As a result of climate change and years of deforestation, diminishing snowfall and the reduction of topsoil, especially in Badghis province, rainfall has run down the mountainsides instead of infiltrating the ground. This intensifies flooding during the rainy season, as rivers are overfilled, and this increases the chance of droughts during the dry season, as groundwater has been depleted. This high level of runoff leads to flooding and loss of life, destruction of property, and prolonged displacement.

These water sources are drying up as population use increases, coupled with a lack of effective water resource management. Following the 2018 drought, in trying to meet the immediate needs of those searching for water, several humanitarian organizations drained and permanently damaged scarce water supplies.

Interventions: addressing both long and short-term goals and reducing disaster risks

During the 2018 drought, World Vision International took an integrated approach to the water crisis in Afghanistan by focusing on short-term and long-term water replenishment. World Vision constructed drinking water networks to meet the immediate water needs of displaced people and created macro-catchments aimed at replenishing the groundwater supply and helping displaced persons return home. Additionally, it focused on developing national policies that protect water resources, emphasizing the prioritization of groundwater recharge.

One of its key developments has been the macro-catchments, which are large water basins built in flood paths to slow down and catch runoff water. By slowing water down, more of the runoff infiltrates groundwater systems, recharging aquifers for later use. A typical large macro-catchment pond is about 60 metres in diameter and can hold 5,600 cubic metres of water, usable both for irrigation and as drinking water.

An assessment of the impact of macro-catchments conducted by World Vision in 2019 in Khwaja Charom village in Qadis District, Badghis Province, found that they not only reduced annual flooding but also raised the water table below the village. Villagers indicated that they had initially thought that the macro-catchment reservoir built nearby would stop flood waters and provide a source of water for irrigation and drinking, but they had not anticipated its impact on the kariz system by raising the water level in their wells (World Vision, 2020).

World Vision confirmed that multiple kariz systems and wells in town that had previously been dry now contained sufficient amounts of usable water. Residents requested additional macro-catchments be built in surrounding villages that were struggling with yearly flooding and lower water tables (World Vision, 2020).

The macro-catchment system was perfectly designed to meet Afghanistan's short- and long-term water issues and reduce flooding risk. The drought in 2018 was severe, but with climate change effects, it is anticipated that several more droughts in the coming decade can be expected. World Vision's response addressed local immediate water needs in IDP camps in Badghis and Herat provinces. It aimed to provide rapid, environmentally sustainable water solutions to help recharge communities' water systems for years and decades to come. These long-term interventions were developed and implemented during the humanitarian crisis.

(Continued)

Box 3.2 Continued

Significant policy changes were needed to confront water availability decreases throughout Afghanistan and to safeguard water resources for future needs. Over the last five years, World Vision International has worked closely with national and local leaders in Afghanistan to address water resource needs and develop a range of climate change adaptations that will mitigate water table decline and enhance local resilience.

In line with this goal, World Vision with other key stakeholders led the development of the government of Afghanistan's new national Operation and Maintenance of Rural Water Systems Strategy. This policy helped the government set minimum standards for humanitarian and development organizations working in WASH in Afghanistan to ensure that water resources are used in sustainable ways. Key components include provisions for climate change mitigation, environmental sustainability, and common benchmarks for foreign organizations and donors working in Afghanistan. These new nationwide policies include definitions for water conservation and environmental sustainability as humanitarian and development priorities. The new policy will help bridge the humanitarian–development divide, guaranteeing that humanitarian and development water interventions prioritize water source conservation and groundwater recharge while seeking to aid those living in emergency contexts. In a similar vein, World Vision is working with the Afghanistan government and other actors to strengthen water governance through groundwater monitoring and regulation.

Box 3.3 Jordan: environmentally sustainable solid waste management project in Azraq camp

World Vision
Acknowledgement: Hasmik Kocharyan

Introduction

In response to the Syrian conflict and refugee crisis, the Jordanian government established the Azraq refugee camp in April 2014, a purpose-built camp for incoming Syrian refugees. The camp, which covers approximately 15 square kilometres, sits about 25 kilometres from the nearest town and has a population of around 36,500 (World Vision, 2019).

World Vision has been providing solid waste management (SWM) services there since 2017, funded by the EU and the German Federal Ministry of Economic Cooperation and Development and implemented through the German Society for International Cooperation. This project was recently renewed in 2020 for another three years.

Jordan 'recycles approximately 7 per cent of the 2 million tons of municipal waste produced annually' (World Vision, 2019). With approximately 650,000 Syrian refugees currently calling Jordan home, managing an already overburdened solid waste system has become more complicated.

Interventions: addressing environmental concerns and sustainability

The key activities of World Vision's SWM programme include:

- providing a two-bin system for recyclable and non-recyclable waste for every eight households;
- a behaviour change campaign for household members to sort materials properly prior to daily collection;
- daily waste collection from households and community centres;
- the construction, maintenance, and running of a solar-powered 'green centre' that sorts and processes daily waste;

(Continued)

Box 3.3 Continued

- 'cash for work' opportunities for Syrian refugees through the hiring of 40 incentive-based volunteers for daily collection and sorting and 150 incentive-based volunteers on a monthly rotation for behaviour change activities (World Vision, 2019).

About 17 tons of waste are generated daily in Azraq camp. World Vision has provided recyclable and non-recyclable waste bins throughout the camp and now collects waste from these bins daily. It is then taken to the green processing plant in the camp by refugees employed by the SWM programme. Over 15 per cent of the collected waste is recyclable and is sorted and then sold to local Jordanian vendors. The proceeds are reinvested in the programme; this currently covers 20 per cent of programme costs. The non-recyclable solid waste then goes to landfill. This environmentally friendly solution reduces the impact the refugee camp has on Jordan and provides a lower cost for programming due to financial recovery through recyclable materials, reducing the burden on foreign investment.

Behaviour change training has been a critical component of this programme. This training focuses on promoting the sorting of waste among families, increasing the amount of correct sorting that takes place before collection. It is anticipated that correct sorting before collection will lead to a higher percentage of recyclable materials going to local business vendors and an increase in recuperated programme costs. More recently, COVID-related safety training has also become part of these behaviour change training sessions.

World Vision is now working on expanding this project with local municipalities. This will allow the programme to continue beyond the humanitarian funding timeline, bridging the humanitarian, development, and peace nexus. Over the last three years, World Vision has built sustainable and cost-effective infrastructure that local municipalities can now maintain and then expand.

Challenges

World Vision faced three key challenges in designing and implementing this programme. The first was around programme design: the original design was even more environmentally sustainable and included a composting component to help fertilize and grow food within the camp. This would have allowed Syrian refugees to establish their own gardens to help supplement their food supply. However, this part of the programme was rejected by the Jordanian government due to the temporary nature of the Azraq camp; only the recycling and SWM components were allowed. At the time of writing, World Vision was conducting an ongoing feasibility study and market analysis concerning the potential of implementing composting in the camp.

Originally, World Vision had planned to build a partnership with a local Jordanian company to collect, remove, and sort the solid waste. However, due to problems with Jordanian laws, which do not allow humanitarian funding to go to private companies, and issues with information sharing and accountability, World Vision was ultimately required to re-envision this programme, building and running the recycling centre and waste collection themselves. This means that the current version of this sustainable solid waste programme relies wholly on humanitarian funding as there are no fees for collecting waste. Therefore, it could not be self-sufficient from a business perspective.

COVID-19 also presented major issues, as daily waste collection increased the potential for its spread throughout the camp. Furthermore, Jordan imposed a nationwide lockdown as part of its COVID response to reduce the virus's spread. However, World Vision was able to obtain police escorts to continue transporting waste from the camp to the landfill site.

Box 3.4 Yemen: rehabilitating water systems for conflict-affected populations

Save the Children
Acknowledgement: Peter Nyamoko

Introduction

Yemen is facing one of the largest single-nation humanitarian crises in the world. According to the 2021 *Humanitarian Needs Overview: Yemen*, 20.7 million people are in need of humanitarian or protection assistance (OCHA, 2021: 4). Since March 2015, the conflict in Yemen has spread to 21 out of 22 governorates. The displacement and hosting of IDPs place a significant burden on families to find scarce food, water, and other resources, particularly shelter, healthcare, education, and essential household items.

Even before 25 March 2015, when the conflict in Yemen escalated, the country faced enormous levels of humanitarian need, with 15.9 million people requiring some kind of humanitarian or protection assistance in late 2014. These needs stemmed from years of poverty, underdevelopment, environmental decline, intermittent conflict, and the weak rule of law, including widespread human rights violations.

The conflict in Yemen has only exacerbated the already scarce water supply. Humanitarian actors in Yemen signed a joint letter stating that:

> Over five years of conflict has damaged water systems, left the health sector on the brink of collapse and led to disease outbreaks, including cholera. It is estimated that up to 70 per cent of Yemenis currently lack access to soap for handwashing and personal hygiene, and 11.2 million lack access to basic water supplies they need to survive. (UNICEF, 2020)

The WHO estimates that more than 50 per cent of healthcare facilities can no longer give adequate care due to losses in vital support, such as fuel and staff (OCHA, 2015). Country-wide, health facilities and staff are suffering directly from the conflict's impact: according to the WHO, 69 health facilities have been damaged or destroyed since March 2015, and approximately 70 per cent of health facilities are understaffed (WHO, 2015). Without humanitarian support, WASH services throughout Yemen would collapse.

Interventions: using sustainable technology and engaging with authorities

Save the Children supported 26 healthcare facilities, of which six were new sites for the community-based management of acute malnutrition and 20 were fixed location healthcare facilities. Fifteen of these required major WASH interventions, including the rehabilitation of latrines and excreta disposal. Basic WASH supplies were also provided quarterly to each of the targeted healthcare facilities. At least two administration staff at each healthcare facility (one male, one female) were trained in plumbing, medical waste management, and infection prevention and control (IPC).

Save the Children has focused on replacing diesel-powered pumps in water systems with solar pumps, which have cheaper running costs for targeted communities. Although more expensive to install, the total cost of solar pumps is typically cheaper after two or three years of operation compared with diesel-powered pumps, including operation and maintenance costs. Key water challenges for communities have included fuel availability and the cost of running pumps, often leading families to seek cheaper, unsafe water sources. However, the installation of solar systems has led to cheaper, more reliable water supplies in affected communities. To date, out of the 39 rehabilitated water systems, 28 have been converted to solar power.

Save the Children has also worked closely with local community leaders to train water management committees that oversee the water systems. Committees have been trained

---

(Continued)

Box 3.4 Continued

on the operation and maintenance of the water systems and how to repair leaks and replace pipe fittings and taps. They have also been given the tools and spares to maintain water systems in the future. An important part of the committees' sustainability has come from work with the local Yemeni water authority to give the committees institutional support, especially in the case of major breakdowns.

Initial delays in local authority approval have had a major impact on the timeline and success of WASH programming in the country. However, Save the Children was committed to building closer ties with local administrators and building mutual trust and strong communication with them. This included joint monitoring and transparency in budgeting. Over time, this has resulted in waiting times for programme approval being significantly reduced and has allowed both sides to see shared success. It has also enabled Save the Children to align programme design to better meet local needs and the longer-term planning goals of local authorities.

Humanitarian and development nexus: wider initiatives

World Vision and Save the Children have attempted to support the humanitarian–development nexus in practical ways in their WASH programming. A key focus for programming is strengthening institutional capacity, environmental monitoring, and institutional WASH strategy frameworks across the region. These initiatives, largely driven by local community actors, have helped humanitarian and development organizations better align programme designs that meet the current and long-term needs of those served while specifically strengthening the sustainable WASH model's institutional and social areas.

Building institutional capacity

Working with local partners and other local stakeholders to critically reflect on their WASH programmes' impact and effectiveness has strengthened institutions' capacity and helped them plan for sustainability. Investments in local partners' ability to evaluate their programmes go beyond donor expectations for monitoring but support these institutions' growth.

Building environmental monitoring

World Vision's national WASH officers throughout the region worked collaboratively to create environmental indicators suited to the country's context. This also supports local capacity but makes environmental considerations key elements of the planning and monitoring process to minimize the programmes' environmental impact.

Developing community-led institutional strength

Designing a regional WASH strategy starts with clear and measurable objectives. Many country-level WASH strategies were developed in countries' national offices in close collaboration with the MENA regional WASH strategy.

Having an overarching WASH strategy across the region allows humanitarian and development initiatives to set the same goals towards a shared vision and identify areas where they can collaborate.

Developing national and regional institutional strength that meets WASH needs in environmentally sustainable ways is difficult in the water-scarce Middle Eastern context. World Vision recently took the lead in partnership with the government of Afghanistan on developing a national strategy for protecting and repairing water systems throughout the country. This has required strengthening water resource monitoring efforts across Afghanistan and needs humanitarian and development organizations acting in the country to adjust their interventions to maintain the longevity of water sources. These standards aim to ensure that WASH interventions are environmentally sustainable even in times of great need. This national strategy has enabled humanitarian and development organizations to unify WASH programme design to meet the needs of IDPs in Afghanistan and address the long-term impact of climate change in the region.

Child-focused WASH interventions

A key programme led by the IRC and connected to the Dutch WASH Alliance and other partners in Ghana was built around the child-friendly design of latrines. Through the Action Research for Learning programme, the NGO New Energy and partners recognized that it is especially difficult for children below the age of six to use latrines, and therefore they were not using them. This realization was community-driven, and partners realized that there was a strong need for further technology development for child-friendly latrines. New Energy and its partners recognized that their current strategy did not adequately address children's needs due to cultural barriers. In Ghana, children often do not use the same latrines as adults as a sign of respect for the elderly. As a result, child-friendly latrines have been developed that are smaller in size and set aside solely for children's use; these are being used and well maintained. Additionally, soakaways have been constructed for latrines and households to reduce stagnant water, which leads to mosquitos. Community involvement – particularly of women and children – in WASH intervention design and implementation was vital to the success of WASH systems in Ghana.

World Vision has collaborated with Sesame Workshop (creators of *Sesame Street*) to produce WASHUP!, a campaign that includes videos, storybooks, games, and educational materials to promote model hygiene attitudes and behaviour among children and in schools, focusing on vulnerable populations (World Vision, 2017). Targeted behaviours include safe and responsible water practices, latrine use and waste management, consistent handwashing and personal hygiene, as well as children supporting and teaching other children about WASH objectives at home, in school, and in the community.

This started as a development programme to bring about change for children in Zambia; it was reformatted in Arabic for displaced children throughout MENA and quickly spread throughout the region to all children. It has since expanded further into sub-Saharan Africa and Latin America (World Vision, 2017). Identifying tools and programmes that work and sensitively adapting them to new settings can be very effective in humanitarian and development contexts.

Integration across the humanitarian and development nexus: lessons learned

One of the big questions we seek to address with this book is when to start the transition from humanitarian WASH to development WASH. The first case study in Nigeria highlights that the decision to start the transition to a more long-term WASH vision can be complicated, especially in conflict contexts. However, although a country may be defined as being in a humanitarian context by funding organizations, some areas within that country may be ready for development well before others. Having a vision, a theory of change, and a flexible funding stream allows implementors to meet local needs by focusing on life-saving interventions where needed and then transitioning towards reconstruction. Non-household settings, such as schools and healthcare facilities, which are discussed in Chapter 4, can play a vital role as transition points, moving WASH services from short-term to long-term considerations.

An underlying theme that runs through the case studies is the need for evidence-based decision making. This is most prominent in the Nigeria case study, where the choice of humanitarian or more developmental responses depended on an analysis of the stability of the area, among other criteria. But all the case studies show a need for the careful weighing up of criteria, whether political, security, social, technological, financial, or environmental, to move from knee-jerk humanitarian or developmental responses to a more nuanced programme. Vital to this development is the role of local community members in leading WASH programming and in highlighting any gaps, especially during transition, that hinder progress and reconstruction. This is key to allowing humanitarian and development WASH initiatives to reach the most marginalized people.

The WASHUP! programme with Sesame Workshop is a case where an innovative and successful programme was taken from one area, adapted and expanded into new and different contexts. This is easy to get wrong, and the world is littered with failed programmes that worked elsewhere. The financial backing, coupled with a strong cultural and social understanding of the new contexts, has made the adaptation successful, not once but several times. It shows that good ideas can be adapted from one side of the humanitarian–development nexus to benefit the other. The humanitarian sector often 'borrows' or adapts ideas from the development sector, and it is usually the richer for it. Careful planning and monitoring help, but a great idea like this should be exploited to its maximum. We must be aware of past failures and try new ideas that can bridge the nexus.

The role of local government in taking on WASH interventions in both the humanitarian and the development sector is vital. Embedding interventions within local government structures will allow for sustainable replication and effective scaling up of WASH infrastructure. The level and degree to which local government stakeholders will be involved inevitably depends on the country context. Regardless, community-level government players should be involved in data collection and monitoring processes during each of the humanitarian, transitional, and development phases of WASH programming. Local-level actors and national government agencies can add WASH data collection to what they are already collecting. This will allow both content and administration processes across the humanitarian–development divide to become more effective by aligning humanitarian and development organizations with relevant government institutions, leading to better planning and collaboration, improving institutional and financial resource allocation in particular, and eventually delivering WASH services that last.

Sustainable WASH in the case studies

Referring back to Chapter 2, this section highlights the five sections of sustainable WASH (the FIETS model) in the case studies.

Financial sustainability

Of the five aspects of the sustainable WASH model, finance is the most difficult to address from a humanitarian perspective. Short timescales of humanitarian funding make long-term support to communities and institutions difficult, but this is vital in encouraging local willingness to pay for and strengthen WASH structures. Nevertheless, the Jordanian SWM programme was able to offset 20 per cent of operating costs by selling recyclable materials to local vendors. Regulations curtailed other efforts, but further studies continue to make the programme more cost-sustainable. This makes it more open to the possibility of blended financing from other sectors. Decisions in the Yemen and Afghanistan programmes to use sustainable options such as solar-powered pumps and macro-catchments have reduced operating costs for communities.

Institutional sustainability

All the case studies showed a strengthening of institutions as a critical part of their programme, whether those institutions were local partners, local authorities, or government ministries. The humanitarian–development nexus compels humanitarians to engage with authorities and their long-term plans.

'Do no harm' is the minimum we must do here so that our emergency work does not trample over the development planning of governments. Many of these case studies, showing effective and innovative approaches to WASH programming, resulted in closer work with the government to influence policy, such as in Afghanistan and Yemen.

Environmental sustainability

This has become the most pressing of the five aspects of sustainable WASH. We can no longer ignore either the direct or indirect environmental consequences of our actions, even in the short term. The Afghanistan case study shows how the careful selection and development of water supplies have a positive impact on aquifers' long-term sustainability. Not all programmes can have as clear-cut an outcome as this. Still, we can identify risks to the environment from proposed projects and look to minimize them. Disaster risk reduction and climate change adaptations will have to be incorporated as considerations in all programming, even if only a negligible risk to the WASH programme is identified from natural hazards or climate change. Almost always, these considerations will lead to improvements in design and implementation to address climate risks or natural hazards. These areas lead humanitarians to consider the longer-term impacts of their programmes and identify more sustainable solutions.

Technological sustainability

We need to be clear on our technology options – what is going to be more sustainable for the community to manage and operate? Solar-powered pumps are an easy choice to make, as in Yemen, even in a highly insecure area – not only were the operational costs lowered, but there was no longer a threat to the water supply caused by the cutting of fuel supplies. Technological sustainability might mean that the project has to bear a higher cost initially if it means a more reliable supply in the longer term. Other technology choices might be influenced by the standardization of components (are spare parts readily available?) and ease of maintenance (can it be repaired by the community or local technicians?).

Social issues

WASH programming without a social component is almost unheard of today. But we have to be wary that our buzzwords and 'business as usual' do not get in the way of real community engagement. All the case studies highlight the need for local input and control over WASH programming at all stages. As we aim to address the needs of people living in crisis, especially conflict, the Nigeria case study highlights that the interconnectedness of needs goes beyond sector silos, and so a multisectoral response is needed.

Addressing people's real concerns, as in Afghanistan and Nigeria, means time spent listening, discussing, and negotiating to realize a project that meets people's needs and involves them in operating and managing the resulting infrastructure. It might mean looking at options that are not typical emergency WASH programming, such as macro-catchments in Afghanistan. It might mean providing a variety of sectoral responses, as in Nigeria. It almost always means strengthening communities in their ability to manage, operate, and maintain the WASH infrastructure across the humanitarian and development nexus.

CHAPTER 4
The role of non-household settings

One of the key 'how' questions around creating sustainable WASH programmes that bridge the humanitarian–development divide is how non-household settings can further strengthen the alignment of humanitarian and development priorities. Access to water, sanitation, and hygiene facilities at home is simply not enough to achieve a sustainable impact. The availability of adequate WASH facilities in schools, for example, is of critical importance to an effective learning environment and the long-term health of students and teachers. Equally important is the availability of WASH facilities in hospitals, health centres, and clinics; this is key to preventing infections and the spread of diseases. In addition, the availability of WASH facilities in settings ranging from workplaces to refugee camps and detention centres is fundamental to the long-term health and resilience of marginalized people impacted by humanitarian crises.

In this chapter, we provide an overview of WASH initiatives in various settings beyond the household and look at their potential role across the three phases of WASH and the impact they can have on people's lives. Also known as WASH away from home, non-household settings focus on different sites, including schools, healthcare facilities, workplaces, temporary-use settings,[1] mass gatherings, and dislocated population settings. This chapter draws from and expands on a publication written by Kendall and Snel (2016) and originally published by the International Water and Sanitation Centre (IRC), which reflected on WASH in non-household settings. Our primary focus here is on schools and healthcare facilities across the humanitarian–development divide. This is followed by a discussion on mass gatherings and their importance in integrated WASH design.

So far, we have not mentioned gender and inclusive, responsive humanitarian actions. Within the context of non-household settings, there is a need to ensure a more accurate understanding of these issues on the ground. For example, sanitation facilities should be gender-friendly, in alignment with menstrual hygiene management (SNV and IRC, 2013), and they should be appropriately designed in schools, healthcare facilities, and other settings. In addition, there should also be a consistent focus on WASH that aligns with disabilities, as this group is often underrepresented but is an important part of the community (Snel, 2015). Within the humanitarian and development context, the role of those who are disabled should be considered implicitly in terms of facility access (Snel et al., 2015). In other words, humanitarian and development non-household settings should plan and implement in a way that benefits all groups within the affected population, in line with a clear analysis of their specific rights, needs, and capacities.

There have been constructive WASH developments in non-household settings, as highlighted in the SDGs, which focus on long-term WASH, as well as SPHERE for short-term WASH. To date, the WASH sector has concentrated on community and household programming and research. WASH in schools started becoming a focus in the 1980s (Snel et al., 2004), followed by WASH in healthcare facilities at the beginning of 2015 (Kendall and Snel, 2016). Much work is still needed to develop a further understanding of these and other non-household WASH settings; this is essential to developing impactful universal WASH coverage across the humanitarian and development spectrum. This chapter fills in critical gaps in the areas of advocacy, the sharing of knowledge, and consensus building, with the aim of increasing harmony between WASH subsectors, leading to more robust integration across the humanitarian–development divide through institutional structural settings that often exist already in both fragile and stable countries.

Temporary learning facilities in humanitarian settings

Education is vital for effective long-term recovery during and after a humanitarian crisis. However, without effective coordination of WASH programmes in schools and temporary learning facilities (including WASH infrastructure and hygiene promotion), there are often too many barriers for students to attend schools safely. There is ample literature on WASH standards in development contexts that relates to permanent education facilities (IRC, 2007). This literature provides guidelines and suggestions for every aspect of WASH programming, including infrastructure, supplies, topics for hygiene promotion, and food safety. However, most indicators, data, and standards have been written and are meant for permanent school facilities. During a crisis, education is often provided through rapidly built temporary learning centres, especially in refugee and IDP contexts. These facilities are designed to prevent a detrimental learning gap until more permanent solutions can be established or constructed. Temporary learning centres are a key feature of refugee and IDP camps. However, as discussed in Chapter 1, humanitarian crises are growing in length and scope. It is vital that humanitarian responders incorporate long-term WASH initiatives in the early design and implementation of temporary learning centres.

Temporary learning centres as part of the humanitarian response enable children to continue preparing for future success. They are often seen in refugee and IDP sites where traditional schools are not available. If present, they are often underfunded and serve large populations. In such contexts, it is not uncommon for temporary learning centres to have inadequate WASH facilities, resulting in long lines, which can lead to reduced time in class, safety concerns for children, and an increase in the spread of disease and illness (Save the Children, 2019). Planning for WASH needs in temporary learning centres must begin before construction, as 'integration of WASH can be difficult if it is not initially in the plans for education' (Save the Children, 2019: 1). Save the Children explained further that:

> WASH is not always discussed in the same context of education for refugees and IDPs and this could impede the meeting of WASH standards in temporary learning facilities. For example, if Temporary Learning Centres are established too far from WASH facilities such as toilets and handwashing stations, this can be a barrier to student attendance. Furthermore, if the refugee or IDP camp is crowded, it may be difficult to construct additional WASH facilities after the learning centre has been constructed. (Save the Children, 2019: 1)

Existing challenges faced in both permanent and temporary learning settings

All schools need to have proper WASH facilities as children will have a better chance to succeed if they are in a clean and hygienic environment. Poorly maintained schools and the absence of proper WASH facilities become health hazards. Furthermore, the lack of private, gendered sanitary facilities leads to weak enrolment and retention of girls; this applies to all settings but is especially difficult in the humanitarian context. This can lead to parents withdrawing girls from school or girls opting to skip school, especially during menstrual cycles. This, among other concerns, contributes to a high dropout rate among adolescent girls. Children have a right to be educated in a happy, healthy, and safe learning environment. Good sanitation and hygiene practices are vital to providing effective long-term learning for children by reducing the spread of diseases and ensuring better health and nutrition for them.

WASH in schools

WASH in schools in stable environments refers to a combination of hardware (technical) and software (human development) components that are necessary to produce a healthy school setting by developing appropriate health and hygiene behaviours. WASH in schools aims to make a visible impact on children's health by improving their hygiene practices while also impacting their families and communities. It also attempts to enhance schools' curricula and teaching methods while promoting hygiene practices and community ownership of water and sanitation facilities. It is based on the belief that children are far more receptive to new ideas and practices and can be influenced to cultivate good personal hygiene habits. The promotion of personal hygiene and environmental sanitation within schools is an ideal opportunity for children to adopt good personal hygiene.

Box 4.1 Iraq: WASH in schools, behaviour change through students, and youth as change agents in Zakho District, Dohuk Governorate, and the surrounding communities

Save the Children
Acknowledgement: Omeed Enwiya

Introduction

The 2020 Iraq Humanitarian Needs Overview highlighted how the 2014–17 conflict continues to affect the physical and mental well-being of millions of Iraqis and has an impact on their living standards and capacity for resilience and recovery, while also exposing them to significant protection concerns. Zakho District in the Dohuk Governorate also hosts more than 100,000 IDPs, adding significant strain to existing schools and health centres.

Schools in the region average 300–400 students per school with 40–50 students per class. They often host multiple shifts of students per school. WASH facilities in schools are often out of service or inadequate for the number of students in attendance. This has a tremendous impact on the quality of WASH services provided to students. In Iraq, maintenance and rehabilitation decisions are centralized at a regional level, which often delays services and impacts the quality of education children receive. Some families and parent–teacher associations are occasionally involved in minor maintenance work. However, parent–teacher associations in Iraq face many challenges that hinder their ability to rehabilitate and maintain WASH facilities in the long run.

Historically, Iraqi parents have rarely attended meetings or followed up on their children's academic engagement and achievement. Additionally, schools are ill equipped to provide support to students who lack strong support from parents. Issues of overcrowding add to the resentment, discrimination, and retaliation among students, resulting in bullying and abuse (both physical and verbal), especially between students from different backgrounds (IDPs and host community, or different ethnicities).

Children's needs are rarely taken into consideration when designing WASH facilities. Several rehabilitated facilities in this district are not used due to inadequate or missing latrines, showers, or handwashing stations. In schools, it is common for these facilities to turn into gathering places for students, which can result in bullying or harassment. This issue is even more significant for people and children living with disabilities.

The Iraqi school system is struggling to decentralize after decades of free, government-provided public education. However, national and regional governments have not been able to financially sustain local schools as they seek to rebuild after years of conflict while also trying to meet local and IDP students' needs. Save the Children has been assisting in decentralizing school management, maintenance, and renovation by empowering local administrators and parent–teacher associations to take more ownership over school priorities. This includes local ownership over the reconstruction and maintenance of WASH systems and enhancing child protection on and around school properties. Save the Children's approach sees children – including displaced persons, returnees, refugees, and locals – as vital change agents who can help with WASH design and safety.

Interventions

Save the Children's focus in Northern Iraq aims to:

1. rehabilitate WASH facilities in schools that are outdated or were never designed with safety in mind, particularly for girls (often, bathrooms have not been segregated by gender, which creates safety risks for girls in schools);
2. empower parent–teacher associations and the children themselves as change agents to help fund renovations and maintain safety on school property;

(Continued)

Box 4.1 Continued

3. ensure a safe, positive learning environment for children in schools by training teachers, parents, and children in learning standards and safety procedures.

Community mobilization is key to the successful decentralization of local schools from government funding. Save the Children aimed to help local school administrators and parent–teacher associations gain more control of WASH and school maintenance needs by mobilizing community members and community funding to renovate WASH facilities and to increase child safety measures on and around school grounds. However, the process of mobilizing community members is not standardized and faces many significant challenges. For example, community mobilization is very effective in Sinjar, a small town in Northern Iraq. There is only one ethnic group living in the town, drastically reducing the challenge of enlisting community support for WASH maintenance and funding for schools. Save the Children was able to mobilize the community to pay US$4–US$5 a month per family for several months to cover the costs of rehabilitating WASH facilities at the school until the director of water for the town could find funding to cover the remaining costs.

In contrast, in larger cities such as Zakho, where there is greater ethnic diversity, it can be difficult to unite communities around school needs that serve these diverse populations. These challenges, however, are not insurmountable. UNICEF has been working in Zakho to decentralize schools from national budgets for the last few years. These consistent efforts have made Save the Children's job of mobilizing parent–teacher associations to meet WASH rehabilitation and maintenance needs much more successful.

Challenges

Iraqi citizens perceive education as one of the key challenges facing community mobilization efforts in Northern Iraq. With the rise of Saddam Hussein in 1979, all schooling was centralized and provided free across the country, paid for using government-controlled oil revenues. Since the fall of Hussein in 2003, oil revenue has declined and is no longer controlled centrally. The Iraqi government faces the need to maintain existing schools and to rebuild many others after decades of conflict, especially in the north. Many community members remember when schools were free and do not understand why they would need to mobilize to cover those costs that the new government can no longer meet.

In Northern Iraq, following the 2017–18 defeat of ISIS, Save the Children started working to rehabilitate schools that had few to no functioning WASH facilities. Also, most coeducational schools lacked gendered bathrooms; this is an issue that disproportionately affects girls, who face safety concerns entering unisex bathrooms. In these conditions, girls often do not come to school during their menstrual cycles and often choose to use bathroom facilities during classroom instruction when they are less crowded, or they leave schools as a group to visit nearby homes to use the bathroom there. This severely reduces the hours of classroom instruction girls have with a teacher and impacts their long-term education. Additionally, bathrooms are overcrowded during breaks, resulting in many boys using public spaces to urinate or defecate, which adds to school uncleanliness and poses additional health risks. Fixing the number and quality of bathrooms with WASH facilities in schools drastically increases the quality of education students receive. This is especially true for girls.

The technical components required include installing proper drinking water, handwashing, and toilet facilities in and around the school compound. The human development components are the activities that promote conditions within the school, including the practices of children and teachers, that help prevent water and sanitation-related diseases and worm infestation. School sanitation and hygiene education depend on a process of capacity enhancement of teachers, education administrators, community members, village/ward water and sanitation committees, public health engineering, rural development departments, non-governmental organizations (NGOs), and community-based organizations (CBOs). It seeks to use water, sanitation, and hygiene learning to link children, their families, and communities.

As the Iraq case study highlights, when WASH facilities are not considered upfront, fall into disrepair, or are inadequate to meet needs, there is a negative impact on the quality of children's education, especially in the case of girls. Community mobilization is vital to overcome these challenges.

Healthcare facilities in both long-term and humanitarian settings

Providing safe WASH conditions is essential to protecting human health, especially during infectious disease outbreaks, including the current COVID-19 outbreak (WHO and UNICEF, 2020: 1). In line with a 2015 study on healthcare facilities[2] (Bartram et al., 2015), the WHO and UNICEF (2019) found that one in four healthcare facilities globally lacked basic water services, and one in eight had no sanitation service. In addition, many healthcare facilities lacked basic amenities for hand hygiene and safe segregation and disposal of healthcare waste. There is also a severe lack of statistics regarding healthcare facilities in emergency contexts. A substantial proportion of facilities have no WASH services, and, when reliability, functionality, and safety are considered, service coverage drops to as little as 50 per cent. Limited WASH services in healthcare facilities require urgent action. Inevitably, the current COVID-19 pandemic has further strained existing WASH services and infrastructure in healthcare facilities (WHO and UNICEF, 2019).

Access to adequate WASH systems in healthcare facilities decreases the risk of visit-related or preventable infections for patients, healthcare staff, and the wider community. Healthcare facilities with WASH programming are characterized by a higher quality of treatment and care, efficiency, increased uptake of health services by the community, improvements in healthcare staff morale, and better dissemination of WASH knowledge to the surrounding population. The impact of WASH services in healthcare facilities is so great that it is a prerequisite for numerous other public health development goals, including universal health coverage and the global reduction in maternal and neonatal deaths.

In a global context, awareness about this often overlooked WASH setting has increased over the past decade, culminating in WHO and UNICEF presenting a global action plan in March 2016 (WHO and UNICEF, 2016). Together, the WASH sector has set a target for attaining universal basic coverage of WASH in healthcare facilities by the year 2030.

Challenges

Any significant change from either the humanitarian or the development sector will require the collaboration of public health leaders, WASH professionals, and government officials. A joint report, written by UNICEF and the WHO, indicated that 'improving services will require a number of elements starting with leadership from the health sector, strong technical inputs from the WASH sector and political commitment from governments dedicated to better health for all' (UNICEF and WHO, 2015: v). To make this happen, significant investment will be required to improve infrastructure. Although many new inexpensive, low-technology solutions may help reduce infection rates, planning for both the immediate future and the long term will be vital to achieving significant national improvements.

There is also discord in the WASH sector and among healthcare facility practitioners concerning regional disparity within countries. Major actors will need to decide whether WASH standards should be the same for a rural clinic as for an urban hospital. Or should rural healthcare facilities be held to lower WASH standards than urban ones? This also raises additional questions around the appropriate level of WASH services for each type of healthcare facility (primary, secondary, and tertiary) and how to differentiate them. To achieve this, each country needs to do a baseline assessment of public and private healthcare facilities, and, if they have not already done so, provide explicit standards for healthcare facilities in different contexts.

Refugee camps in humanitarian and longer-term settings

Displaced populations are growing internationally. In emergencies, refugees and IDPs, often as large groups of exhausted people, likely with very few personal items, are relocated to a previously uninhabited area. Refugees and IDPs find themselves fleeing from negative circumstances in their homelands only to encounter sometimes equally difficult situations in the camps.

In refugee and IDP contexts, poor-quality stretches of land are developed quickly to become densely populated, while immediate infrastructure is set up for services to ensure residents' health and safety. Even in these challenging settings, refugees and IDPs have a human right to drinking water and sanitation. The fact is that these camps house large populations living together in close temporary quarters for an indeterminate period of time, making them susceptible to the rapid spread of pathogens and other environmental health-related crises. There is a well-established global policy environment for WASH in refugee and IDP camps. Specifically, UN member countries have strong policies concerning refugee and IDP camps and human rights. While the need for WASH programming in these settings has been well publicized in many global campaigns, advocacy needs to continue at the global, regional, and local levels.

The current international policy environment for WASH programming in these settings makes it possible for numerous powerful international and national actors to act together quickly to provide basic services to refugees and IDPs. In the *Camp Management Toolkit*, it states that:

> The most severe internally displaced persons (IDPs) emergencies will usually trigger an international response. The Camp Management Agency as well as the WASH services providers and other operational entities including national authorities, will align WASH-related response activities in strategic partnership with United Nations Children's Fund (UNICEF) as the Global WASH Cluster under the Inter-Agency Standing Committee (IASC) cluster approach. Refugee emergencies are coordinated through the UN Refugee Agency (UNHCR). (IOM et al., 2015: 203)

Just as stakeholders have their defined roles in emergencies, policy clearly sets out the acceptable conditions that emergency aid must provide. Since its first publication in 2011, the authoritative guidelines for all aspects of refugee and IDP camps, including WASH facilities and services, have been outlined in *The Sphere Handbook: Humanitarian Charter and Minimum Standards in Humanitarian Response* (Sphere Association, 2018). Under the Sphere Project's guidance, international stakeholders have established a set of minimum WASH standards for refugee and IDP camps. Key indicators include the following:

> All groups within the population have safe and equitable access to WASH resources and facilities, use the facilities provided and take action to reduce public health risk; all WASH staff communicate clearly and respectfully with those affected and share project information openly with them, including knowing how to answer questions from community members about the project; there is a system in place for the management and maintenance of facilities as appropriate, and different groups contribute equitably; and all users are satisfied that the design and implementation of the WASH programme have led to increased security and restoration of dignity. (Sphere Project, 2011: 89)

Sphere standards and WASH indicators must be respected in order to ensure displaced persons' rights to live in safety and dignity. They also help measure the impact and effectiveness of humanitarian interventions. At the start of WASH response operations, the setting of indicators to achieve standards must be addressed. Coordination and agreement on indicators are typically carried out at the national level by the WASH and the camp coordination and camp management clusters, and in consultation with relevant authorities, the displaced population, and WASH service providers (IOM et al., 2015).

Challenges

WASH programming in refugee and IDP camps often does not have adequate hardware or software to ensure camp occupants' well-being or prevent potentially devastating epidemics. Immediate action is needed as WASH-related infrastructure often fails to work or does not exist. As noted by Mercy Corps:

> Settings with ongoing social unrest due to war or civil disorder are typically characterized by a breakdown of basic services, including water and sanitation. This is always the case during the first stages of a refugee or IDP scenario, and addressed as part of the immediate package of services that NGOs implement. However, WASH programs in refugee or IDP camps are often insufficient to meet the minimum standards. (Mercy Corps, 2008: 3)

WASH contexts and conditions vary between camps – and, in some cases, within refugee camps. Further development is required to ensure that a high standard of WASH services is delivered across varying camp settings and contexts.

Box 4.2 Myanmar: multisectoral approach to WASH in emergencies

Save the Children
Acknowledgement: Thaw Si Htin Zaw

Introduction

In Rakhine State, intercommunal violence in 2012 led to the displacement of approximately 145,000 people. At the end of 2019, some 130,866 IDPs were still in camps in Central Rakhine, of which about 78 per cent were women and children. In addition, an estimated 470,000 non-displaced stateless Rohingya and 117,000 people from non-Rohingya communities are estimated to need humanitarian support. The episode of violence in northern Rakhine State in 2017 led to the cross-border displacement of around 790,000 Rohingya to Bangladesh. Until the return process is shown to be safe and voluntary, it is unlikely that this group will return, but negotiations continue between the governments in Myanmar and Bangladesh.

The Advisory Commission on Rakhine State (2017) called for the IDP camps' closure and for the government to take greater responsibility for supporting the Rohingya and other displaced populations. The Ministry of Health and Sports has been one of the more active ministries in implementing the recommendations, including the development of an action plan. In 2020, the State Health Department recruited 53 Muslim auxiliary midwives and delivered a number of training sessions to build community health workers' capacity. In addition, 130 additional midwives were recruited for the state. The Department also implemented the Integrated Management of Acute Malnutrition, including initiating mother–child cash transfers inside and outside the camps to support mothers financially during the first 1,000 days of a child's life (Advisory Commission on Rakhine State, 2017).

Rakhine State's context is complex, with intercommunal violence occurring against a backdrop of significant poverty and underdevelopment. Rakhine has some of the lowest social and economic indicators in Myanmar (World Bank Group, 2014). While data and indicators are patchy, and coverage of healthcare and sanitation in Rakhine is extremely limited, it is known that chronic and acute malnutrition levels are the highest nationally (FAO, 2019). Rakhine State is also susceptible to recurrent natural hazards such as severe storms (cyclones), flooding, and mudslides. People in Rakhine State have been affected

(Continued)

Box 4.2 Continued

by recurring intercommunal violence, a historical and political phenomenon closely linked to identity and citizenship. Tensions between Muslim and Buddhist populations escalated in violent clashes in 2012, resulting in nearly 140,000 people being displaced, including over 50,000 children under 18.

Intervention

In terms of logistics, since 2013 the WASH team has participated in monthly camp coordination and camp management meetings, organized by the Danish Refugee Council and Lutheran World Federation, where operational and programmatic issues are discussed. A State Health Department meeting shared updated COVID-19 information and the new procedure for travelling allowance processes. Since 2013, Save the Children's WASH programme has actively participated in the WASH cluster meetings and in technical working group meetings in Sittwe. When working from home during the pandemic, WASH senior staff coordinate with the internal regional management team, sharing programme updates, COVID-19 information, and remote implemented activities, and discussing effective integration and collaboration in their respective activities. This coordination is run through local committees that oversee WASH facilities, and community volunteers assist in hygiene promotion sessions. Connecting international support with local community leadership allows for better contextualization and a stronger connection to those living in acute need.

The Rakhine programme continues to cover people's needs in Pauktaw and Sittwe camps, where Save the Children has been operating since the beginning of 2013, focusing on improving nutrition security and contributing to a reduced risk of mortality and morbidity due to diarrhoeal diseases. A vital component of nutrition programming is the prevention of life-threatening acute malnutrition, and an essential element of service integration is to ensure that the root causes of each child's malnutrition have been addressed. Child malnutrition in this context is linked to a lack of access to water and sanitation, which puts children at a high risk of diarrhoea and water-borne diseases. Therefore, Save the Children's focus has been on delivering safe drinking water throughout the camps by monitoring water sources, thereby improving camp members' overall health. This is connected to messaging around WASH, nutrition and health services, and best practices. By coordinating WASH and nutrition specifically, Save the Children has been able to link messaging and is better able to reach marginalized populations. Due to the equally fundamental impact WASH can have on addressing the causes of malnutrition, Save the Children therefore delivered an integrated Nutrition–Health–WASH intervention in specific camps, addressing WASH needs and incorporating hygiene promotion sessions in antenatal support and infant and young child feeding centres.

The WASH situation is relatively stable in Sin Tet Maw camp, where latrines and water supply are in place and running well. The project has continued to ensure that latrines are adequate in quantity and designed so that excreta is sealed from the environment and treated when pit latrines are full. Save the Children has integrated hygiene promotion focused on handwashing with soap and water and has also ensured that access to water is sufficient and safe even during the dry season and that hygiene practices are maintained. Save the Children's core life-saving nutrition and WASH activities have been prioritized for this phase, but to ensure that the project is also conflict-sensitive, Save the Children has addressed some WASH issues such as water quality and access to latrines in the surrounding villages, in continuation of previous phases of intervention. Furthermore, women, especially pregnant women, are targeted explicitly with nutrition sessions and proper WASH behaviour training to improve personal hygiene and sanitation practices.

(Continued)

Box 4.2 Continued

IDPs still face significant challenges in accessing quality, equitable healthcare and nutrition services from the formal health sector, especially for basic emergency obstetric and new-born care, childbirth care, and emergency services. The Rakhine IDP camps are overcrowded, with populations living in extremely poor conditions. While the most vital water and sanitation infrastructure is in place, it requires constant renovation, maintenance, and support to ensure that it is used and managed properly. Save the Children runs its WASH programming through a multisectoral strategy in which WASH, nutrition, and health staff are all working together to achieve individual sectoral outcomes.

Integration between WASH and other sectors, such as health and nutrition, is vital to reach sustainable outcomes. Although the case study above is not new in the way that Save the Children is integrating WASH with nutrition, it highlights the compatibility between these sectors and shows that they can work together to reach desired outcomes. The connections between WASH and nutrition allow for shared interventions and outcomes, and a unified institutional and social community-led response.

Mass gatherings

Mass gatherings such as large-scale religious festivals often have weak existing WASH infrastructure that is insufficient to accommodate the massive numbers of visitors safely. In most cases, temporary facilities are installed to make basic services available to visitors. However, such gatherings can also be extremely useful platforms to sensitize thousands of people to relevant WASH issues and introduce WASH programming.

The overcrowding, difficult management, and temporary circumstances of mass gatherings make them breeding grounds for public health threats. Visitors are especially susceptible to water-borne diseases, so access to safe WASH services is important in preventing potential outbreaks.

However, these settings, in both humanitarian and development contexts, give organizers the unique opportunity to educate visitors on the importance of WASH services and allow them to experience programming through the use of appropriate technologies and interactive training in safe WASH practices. Attendees can take this knowledge back home and share it with friends and family.

The policy environment in relation to organized mass gatherings depends on the nature of the gathering and varies from country to country. Nevertheless, there is typically a clear responsibility for WASH in these settings. For the Kumbh Mela, a Hindu pilgrimage and festival in India, the district where it takes place (alternating between four locations every 12 years) is responsible for WASH for pilgrims. Civil society organizations also contribute. For the Hajj, an annual pilgrimage to Mecca in Saudi Arabia, an organizing committee is dedicated to the planning and provision of WASH facilities for pilgrims. In these cases, WASH-related policy is well established and a priority for event leaders.

In reality, it is hard to enforce and evaluate the greater policy environment for this particular WASH setting because of the diverse nature of mass gatherings. The examples given are two of the largest mass gatherings globally, and they are both related to religious celebrations. They are also the subject of the most research and academic publications. So, conclusions about the policy environment for WASH programming at mass gatherings based solely on these two examples would misrepresent aspects of these types of settings.

Monitoring and evaluation in these settings remain very basic; professionals working in this area are still focusing on the best way to gain insights into WASH in these settings and how to overcome the challenges of the number of people involved. The most popular methods used so far are qualitative: visual observations made by researchers and interviews with visitors. A publication by Singh and Bisht (2014), focusing on the Kumbh Mela in 2013, reflected on strategic measures around quantitative WASH indicators, such as testing surface water for the total faecal coliform count. Another study of the same mass gathering included standard WASH indicators such as microbiological water quality testing of potable water supply and the number of latrines to attendees.

This brief focus on some non-household settings can provide an insight into further bridging the gap between the WASH humanitarian and development sectors. More work in terms of evidence-based, practical research needs to take place. Still, we should be aware that, by working with and through existing non-household institutional settings, we can create far more efficient and effective WASH services that last.

Notes

1.   Temporary settings can include restaurants, accommodation, transportation hubs, transportation vehicles, markets, places of worship, and public WASH facilities, among others.
2.   In 2015, WHO and UNICEF conducted the first worldwide survey of WASH in healthcare facilities (HCFs). Data was collected on WASH conditions in 66,101 HCFs across 54 low- and middle-income countries. The report found that 38 per cent of HCFs did not have improved water sources, 19 per cent did not have improved sanitation, and 35 per cent did not have water and soap for handwashing.

CHAPTER 5
Moving forward: bridging the divide

How do we bridge the WASH humanitarian–development divide? As we have highlighted throughout this book, there is no easy answer. Here, however, we hope to highlight some positive trends that are taking the WASH sector forward. Effectively bridging the nexus will require more than just following these trends; it will also require intentional shifts in how we address challenges and unify programme design to meet the needs of the most marginalized and in how we train and hire the next generation of humanitarian and development professionals. Portions of the section on humanitarian/development workers of the future draws from and expands upon a paper we published with *Waterlines* in October 2020 (Sorensen and Snel, 2020). We connect that argument with further conversations we have had with other WASH professionals since then.

Public health/WASH in healthcare facilities, schools, refugee camps, and other institutions

In terms of the potential role of non-household settings, donors play a determining part and can emphasize the need to provide WASH support. Until recently, donors have held a narrow view of what constitutes an 'emergency' activity and what constitutes a 'development' activity, regardless of the context. For example, very few donors have defined emergency WASH in schools as part of relevant humanitarian activities.[1] Due to this discrepancy, it is rare to see emergency WASH funding going into schools. WASH funding in schools is still heavily skewed towards development contexts. Although these settings are considered long-term institutions, their importance early in emergency contexts necessitates an earlier response to ensure a quick transition towards development.

Another example in refugee settings is where the long-term trucking of water is the norm, but it becomes costly if maintained for long periods of time. However, built infrastructure such as pipes, tanks, tap stands, and even macro-catchments, as highlighted in the Afghanistan case study, would be much cheaper in the long run and would leave infrastructure behind after the emergency, which would be much more realistic and sustainable. It is vital to have an early assessment of water supply options and a refugee settlement's sustainability if it were to function without a long-term water supply. Trucking water while rehabilitating or building infrastructure would be needed. But, in many cases, such a long-term vision is required early in an emergency and is often missing. This is outside ongoing complexities regarding politically sensitive issues in line with providing temporary housing for refugees where no permanent infrastructure can be put in place.

Vocational training and long-term planning to assist in financing and maintaining refugees' and IDPs' livelihoods after their initial displacement are needed, especially when the average refugee or IDP remains in a camp for around 20 years. Although vocational and livelihoods assistance in refugee and IDP contexts is often politically complicated, ideally long-term camps and settlements should be designed in close coordination with development actors. These camps often become new cities and would be best served by connecting them to local WASH infrastructure. Commencing this work with local WASH authorities and utility organizations on day one in a refugee or IDP camp will ensure long-term functionality. One example highlighted in the Jordan case study looked at the Azraq Syrian refugee camp, where the camp was purposefully designed with long-term considerations in mind. When initiated during the emergency phase, capacity building of technical staff creates stronger links for development when the transition phase begins. In other words, designing programmes that establish services and management models that can be handed over when transitioning to long-term development is an institutionally sound solution. This requires local and national government support to succeed. An increased focus on advocacy work aimed at resilience building in disaster-prone countries will go a long way towards reducing risk and fostering preparedness through government rather than international funding streams.

WASH is more than just water service delivery; it is a major contributing factor in facilitating child protection, education, health, and economic recovery. When there is strong intersectoral coordination with a strategic, adequate, coherent, and effective response to a humanitarian crisis, with a vision for the transition to development, everyone wins. A holistic approach is necessary but often problematic in humanitarian and development responses. Integrated programming in a humanitarian context takes the form of shared baseline studies, monitoring and evaluation, and learning from outcomes between organizations, governments, other partners, and stakeholders serving the same affected population. Clusters and other coordination mechanisms should be key forums for instigating and strengthening these initiatives.

Focusing on the whole water and sanitation chain usually helps resolve small, unsustainable, isolated interventions. This entails thinking outside one's own organization and sector. Activities that facilitate interactions and coordination are vital, as is undertaking quality monitoring at all stages of the chain (from access to facilities to environmental safety and actual use by communities). This integrated approach works when forming or strengthening partnerships within international, national, and local institutions or organizations that work not just in WASH but also in the health, education, child protection, and livelihoods sectors.

WASH delivery through the sustainable WASH model

In bridging the humanitarian–development divide, it is critical to have political willingness and financial resources with a sound institutional setup connected to a clear understanding of social context and environmental sustainability at the national, regional, and global level. There is nothing more important in making the humanitarian and development WASH sector work more effectively and efficiently. To continue to move forward, we need to consistently reflect on the sustainable WASH model with a clear transitional vision across the three phases of WASH.

Sustainable WASH, as noted previously, relies on good governance leading to strong local and national policy that provides and protects water resources, especially for poor, marginalized populations. Howard et al. (2020) discussed how the COVID-19 outbreak has made water treatment a priority:

> [H]owever, there is little evidence for policy responses to increase access to, or reduce intermittence in, supply that would support households in accessing sufficient water and sustaining the handwashing required. Reliance on communal water sources lessens the ability to adopt physical distancing and prevents households reliant on such sources from self-isolating. These are policy failures within the WaSH sector and in wider public policy. They arise from structural deficiencies that result in poor planning, weak governance, mis-focused prioritisation and under-investment. Financing instruments that could help reduce inequalities in service provision should be urgently considered. (Howard et al., 2020: 625)

In humanitarian contexts with multiple independent actors, policy failures only amplify WASH service disparities. Government policy, both local and national, is the natural coordinating framework that leads to sustainable WASH interventions that last.

Although the WASH sector as a whole is not necessarily very advanced in building bridges between the humanitarian and development realms, as noted at the Stockholm International Water Institute (SIWI) World Water Week (German WASH Network, 2019), there are currently many new initiatives that are building momentum. The most recent 'Triple Nexus in WASH' meeting, which took place in February 2021 and was organized by the Global WASH Network, showed that key actors including the Global WASH Cluster, Sanitation and Water for All (SWA), UNICEF, and UNHCR, among others, are willing to come to the table and reflect more creatively on sustainable WASH services across the humanitarian–development divide. This is highlighted further with the current reformulation of the SWA Partnership strategy (SWA, 2020b), which is now providing a window of opportunity to harmonize frameworks between SWA and the Global WASH Cluster.

In other words, the WASH sector is now, more than ever, engaged in wider discussions about WASH system strengthening. An increasing number of organizations are developing a long-term vision for water and sanitation services and are looking in a more systematic way at how they work in fragile contexts (German WASH Network, 2019). However, the COVID-19 pandemic has made this a compelling time. As Howard et al. argue:

> COVID-19 reminds us that hygiene, safe water and sanitation are essential to protect human life. Short-term action should rapidly ensure that everyone can access sufficient water and soap to practice good hygiene and hygiene facilities are available in all public places. In the medium term, a priority is reliable sustained water supplies and sanitation systems that meet enhanced SDG targets, as we propose here. In the long term, WASH systems must be sustainable and resilient to future threat, including those associated with climate change, and contribute to preparedness for, prevention of and response to pandemic disease. (Howard et al., 2020: 626)

The COVID-19 outbreak, together with climate change, make this an especially important opportunity for both the humanitarian and the development WASH sectors to strengthen synergies and maximize their full potential. The most recent SWA report on the Finance Ministers' Meetings states that:

> climate crisis is affecting access to services through extreme weather events and changes to patterns of rainfall and water resources, and the impact is being felt particularly by the most vulnerable and disadvantaged populations. Resilience must be designed into all services in order to ensure that they remain sustainable and reach everyone. (SWA, 2020b)

However, in an interview, a former key humanitarian WASH UNICEF staff member indicated that climate change currently seems to be a competing agenda, and this perspective does a real disservice to the WASH sector.[2] If climate change, at all levels, were aligned with the peace nexus, this could provide the key united front that brings the humanitarian and development WASH sectors together. Topics such as water resource management in extreme droughts and floods can be fundamental ways forward for the next generation of professionals. In other words, the WASH sector is increasing in importance as the challenge of global climate change becomes the central issue of future humanitarian and development responses.

With regard to the sustainable WASH model in the sustainable delivery of services, there are a number of positive initiatives taking place at the global, regional, and national political levels, as mentioned in this publication. However, these initiatives currently require national governments to drive the change towards a successful, holistic, integrated, and sustainable future. This is made clear by a survey responder and former Water, Engineering and Development Centre (WEDC) colleague, who stated:

> This in turn means a far stronger advocacy to reflect on financial streams and how donor funding is currently being funnelled in the

humanitarian and development sector around WASH. Increasing WASH funding on health grounds implicitly implies a reduction in other health spending – especially on drugs that are not as cost-effective as public health measures. Instead of health sector being an ally, it could be seen as the sector prioritizing cure rather than care – expensive medical treatments over prevention. This has been shown in this time of COVID, with little behaviour research carried out compared with curative responses. The evidence supports environmental health measures, but funding decisions do not necessarily follow evidence, as is clear from past WASH experiences.[3]

The critical question now is who should be in the driving seat moving forward – from the humanitarian or the development side of the WASH sector? Emergency staff are well aware of the divide but often lack the skills or mandate to focus on building bridges. At the same time, development leaders have often avoided this discussion. However, due to their skilled international, regional, and local staff, they are far better equipped to deal with the challenges of bridging this divide. Although the bridging will be tenuous, it would be much better to promote early engagement by development actors in an emergency rather than expect humanitarian workers to independently look beyond immediate or short-term interventions.

Integrated WASH programme design

In INGOs such as Save the Children or World Vision, there is a stronger focus on combining different aspects such as nutrition, education, and child protection programming with improved water, sanitation, and hygiene access. This helps allow more people within and across communities and nations to access improved WASH services. However, there is currently a key gap, both a technical and an organizational disconnect, between WASH and various other thematic areas.

Integrated WASH programming will require systematic alignment between multisectoral organizations and inter-sectoral ministries, with all working towards a shared vision for emergency response, recovery, development, and future resilience. External factors from climate change to food insecurities will continue to force WASH professionals to move more quickly, given the urgency of these situations. This, in turn, means recognizing key external factors such as fragile contexts, socio-economic and political tensions, water scarcity due to climate change, and food insecurity, and how they are all connected to and impact emergency and long-term WASH programming. Hence, the integrated role of WASH and public health or WASH and nutrition will be far more visible in the coming year (Bill and Melinda Gates Foundation, 2020). Non-household settings and integrated programming will play a vital role in future WASH developments, including in developing an ongoing response to pandemic outbreaks.

Building frameworks for integrated WASH programming with other key sectors is a crucial step as we move forward. This type of integration requires a reimagining of the way in which humanitarian sectors and development organizations work together. Among other changes, this requires rethinking how data is created and shared and how organizations collaborate to meet challenges during the humanitarian response. Developing reliable data based on research in humanitarian settings is critical for moving the sector forwards. Developing more evidence of success will require a greater commitment by humanitarian organizations and responders to conduct and produce research that goes beyond the typical aid reports that focus simply on what happened and what was delivered.

One example of sectors working together to better meet the needs of those living in humanitarian settings is the joint operational framework between the Global Health Cluster and the Global WASH Cluster (Global Health Cluster and Global WASH Cluster, 2020). This framework, which focused on combating the spread of cholera, is a perfect example of the inter-sectoral nature of WASH and also highlights the value that can be achieved by different humanitarian sectors integrating their programming to meet humanitarian challenges better. This framework could be used as a template to integrate humanitarian WASH with other sectors' priorities, including nutrition, health, food security, and safety, to name just a few. Furthermore, these frameworks should be developed as an integrated tool between humanitarian sectors and across the humanitarian, development, and peace nexus. Agreements between the humanitarian WASH sector, development organizations, and government institutions strengthen the effectiveness of WASH in emergencies by creating intentional WASH programming with a plan for the transition to long-term development. Deliberate foresight by humanitarian WASH actors breaks down the barriers between the humanitarian, development, and peace sectors.

The humanitarian/development workers of the future

What does all this mean for the next generation of humanitarian and development workers? Predictions made by various professionals state that, over the next 10 years, the humanitarian and development field will face significant changes as new skills, expanded technologies, shifting funding streams, and growing complexity all collide within the sector.[4] This will require professionals to be even more open-minded, proactive, and innovative to remain successful. Additionally, this will require teams, especially in multi-mandated organizations, to reimagine their systems, organizational structures, implementing principles, and expectations in ways that promote 'collaborative co-production' between teams and lead to new shared outcomes (Fanning and Fullwood-Thomas, 2019). This cooperation will have to move beyond just humanitarian and development sectors and include partnerships with researchers (Saywell and Crocker, 2019), leading to a better grasp of bottlenecks and long-term learning as the WASH sector embraces the changes needed to meet future challenges. WASH professionals will have to reflect critically on their role in the sector as they consider new skills sets and links between external factors and their impact on WASH programming. These external factors will require specialized knowledge to be managed effectively and will include issues such as disease outbreaks, climate change, food insecurities, and protracted war crises.

A survey by Devex (2018) of humanitarian and development practitioners found that developing new skills and competencies with technology will be vital for practitioners to thrive in the next decade and beyond; this relates especially to tools such as geographic information systems (GIS), artificial intelligence (AI), and big data.[5] A practitioner's success in the future will be significantly enhanced if they have the ability to learn and utilize new technologies in programme design and implementation. As the challenges faced by humanitarian and development workers grow, these tools will be critical to continue making the impact governments and organizations aim to create. However, more important than just learning to apply these tools in humanitarian and development contexts is the ability to integrate technology with collaboration between humanitarian and development organizations, governments, and other external partners. This collaboration will require the next generation of development workers to acquire the substantial technical understanding needed in the WASH sector, including engineering, construction, risk management, and financing structures. But it will also require investment in soft skills such as communication, adaptability, creativity, and innovation to meet future challenges.[6]

In a discussion of what they see future WASH professionals looking like, a survey respondent and WASH practitioner working with the ICRC indicated:

> Future WaSH practitioner would have to work in a more multidisciplinary world (which – more than now – includes economics, protection ...) and be aware of the complexity of the technical challenge (WaSH systems are per se complex and fragile, technology – AI, IoT (Internet of Things), big data – helps but creates systems which are more complex to handle) and the role of the climate and environmental risks (water scarcity among all). Many other sectors intersecting with the WaSH are growing too. For example, the health sector, increasingly taking into account the mental health components. To succeed, s/he will have to be able to strike a balance among these different challenges and not [lose] track of the humanitarian principles.

Therefore, balance is essential for those working in the WASH sector to navigate growing complexity while working in more complicated, protracted emergency contexts. Finding this balance will determine success in the future.

The next 15–20 years will also see significant adjustments to financing streams as development work becomes more competitive and humanitarian responses become longer and harder to sustain. These growing challenges will push current and new professionals to cooperate more closely with other implementers and build vital new partnerships, especially with actors in the private sector. New financial models, such as impact investing, blended finance, and development impact bonds, which will be vital to success, are more complicated than traditional funding streams that humanitarian practitioners are accustomed to (Smith, 2018a). In other words, the next generation will need to come to the table with a broader range of skills, including business knowledge and experience, and utilize these tools to effectively respond to the complex challenges they will face (Smith, 2018b). In this regard, the future WASH professionals who are likely to be most in demand will be integrators – individuals with strong competencies in multiple sectors across the humanitarian and development spectrum who will have the knowledge and skills necessary to implement life-saving humanitarian responses that still have long-lasting, sustainable impact years later. These individuals will be ideally qualified to coordinate between humanitarian, development, and government responders and foster a collaborative bridge across the triple nexus (Smith, 2018a). For some seasoned humanitarian workers – but not necessarily all – some of this change may be painful and unwanted. Integration is not just about acquiring skills but about approaching change, and the future, with a proactive attitude, open to the potential of innovation.

An essential focus in the coming years will be the further strengthening of national WASH professionals and WASH cluster coordination in line with other countries' humanitarian and development platforms. Not only will future WASH professionals need to be integrators who are well versed in new, essential technologies; they will also need to be well connected with the local context and have the ability to transition between humanitarian, development, and national government priorities. It is vital for these national experts to understand the United Nations Cluster and SPHERE systematic response and to connect emergency responses with local government priorities along with the SDGs and SPHERE standards. This will require a significant strengthening of national WASH coordination structures.

This new generation of WASH professionals will achieve success because they will more likely be local community members who understand the context, and also because they have a strong background in the skills discussed above. There is an ongoing localization/decolonization movement currently taking place (A4EP, 2021). In the future, WASH practitioners will need to know more about the enabling environment and WASH governance along with a strong focus on creating sustainable service delivery models for WASH services, building resilience, and strengthening systems. SIWI has recently developed a paper 'that provides practical guidance for decision-makers and practitioners on how action-oriented water governance processes can be meaningfully designed and, ultimately, how to strengthen efforts aiming to improve water governance' (Jiménez et al., 2020). However, there is still a vital need for further development around water governance and the ways in which governments can mobilize and sustainably reach SDG 6 (Jiménez et al., 2020).

We see a future in which the humanitarian WASH practitioner's primary focus will still be on saving lives. But, by necessity, they will be required to save lives while strengthening the resilience of the WASH sector to ensure predictable emergency responses and protecting gains towards the SDGs. This will need synergies to be built between acute humanitarian situations, protracted contexts, and the development sector by focusing on humanitarian WASH programme designs with long-term perspectives built in, including preparedness, transitions, and resilience across the humanitarian, transitional, and development spectrum.

Advocacy for preparedness and localization is a critical element of future WASH policies and strategies, including system strengthening, especially in fragile contexts. Good governance prior to disasters and conflict is key to reducing the effect emergencies have on people's lives, particularly the poor, who are often impacted the hardest. Developing better collaboration between humanitarian and development actors will go a long way towards efficient humanitarian WASH support. This will involve better communication between humanitarian, development, and government entities about transitions, long-term goals and expectations, and exit strategies. Creating more flexible and multi-annual funding opportunities in partnership with donors and breaking down funding silos between the humanitarian and development sectors make the transition from WASH programming to government and development organizations smoother; this in turn reduces costs and ensures that marginalized groups are not left out.

Finally, this all requires the proactive development of stronger sector coordination platforms, involving humanitarian, development, and government leaders. These platforms will help improve information management and sharing: for example, they will make WASH and health data available and more easily accessible, allowing for better integration across sectors and more substantial alignment between multiple organizations and across the humanitarian–development spectrum.

Successful WASH practitioners will realize that the sustainable management and use of climate-resilient water and sanitation services ensure that human rights relating to water and sanitation are respected at all times, including during and after natural and human-made disasters. They will need to succeed in system strengthening, building a holistic understanding of WASH systems and identifying and working on the barriers that block the realization of inclusive, sustainable, and universal access to WASH services.

Beyond basic technical aspects, there is a need to focus more on combining humanitarian activities with development; this can reduce financial costs and helps create more effective WASH responses with better long-term functionality and an improved return on investment. The consideration of climate change, as well as the governance of water utilities, for example, would therefore become a compulsory part of professional capacity building. This would entail a three-way balancing act between a basic understanding of water supply and sanitation, a background in engineering and public health, various modalities of programming WASH, and, finally, a knowledge of WASH behaviour change programme design and implementation.

Finding this balance between so many different skills sets and knowledge areas in any one person is impossible. A survey respondent working at World Vision stated that:

> WASH has many different facets. It is not possible to be highly skilled in every area. A WASH practitioner should therefore be skilled at bringing people with different specialist skills together to achieve a well-rounded WASH programme. WASH practitioners should also be capable enough to know how to respond to a range of different scenarios. As we are seeing, the spaces in which we operate are becoming less and less predictable. Rather than using standardised approaches, based on scenarios, we have to adapt based on people's actual needs.

The key priority for humanitarian and development organizations has been – and will continue to be – to learn and adapt in alignment with bringing the right sets of skills together. This includes not just technical skills but contextual skills. The next generation of professionals will require the ability to critically think across multiple themes and will have to know how to reprioritize issues as contexts rapidly change, as humanitarian situations so often do. Expanding on this point, a survey respondent working with Oxfam indicated that the WASH sector will require:

> Highly skilled and experienced people who can bring their knowledge to support local staff and local partners to respond to future emergencies. They will be able to advise local organisations and local government at the same time. This entails exceptional people skills to be able to train and support/encourage/advise local people in-country.

Successful humanitarian and development WASH now and in the future requires bringing large groups of diverse, highly skilled individuals together across multiple sectors to accomplish a life-saving and long-lasting impact in the lives of those devastated by natural and artificial disasters. This scale of response requires massive coordination, not just from the top down, but with community input around an immediate and long-term vision for what WASH can do and how it can be done. All of this will entail further crucial capacity building at local, national, and regional levels. Currently, there is insufficient capacity in the humanitarian and development sectors to meet today's WASH needs, let alone future challenges.

This is a daunting vision for the future, not just for the WASH sector but for humanitarian, development, and government progress. Collaboration and trust are going to be the great welders, bringing the humanitarian and development nexus together. As a final thought, Tim Marshall, in his book *Prisoners of Geography*, stated:

> When we are reaching for the stars, the challenges ahead are such that we will perhaps have to come together to meet them: to travel the universe ... as representatives of humanity. But so far, we are still imprisoned in our own minds, confined by our suspicion of the 'other', and thus our primal competition for resources. (Marshall, 2015: 287)

In this respect, there is still a way to go in bridging the WASH humanitarian–development divide. Still, progress is being made and – as individuals and as one collective team of WASH professionals – we move forward together.

Notes

1. At the 2019 UNC (University of North Carolina) Water and Health Conference, Save the Children was asked by UNICEF to do a brief presentation on temporary learning settings in a session on schools and healthcare facilities in which it was clear that this area of work needed far more attention (Weber, 2019).
2. Interview conducted by Mariëlle Snel and Nikolas Sorensen, 23 February 2021.
3. Email exchange with Mariëlle Snel, 24 November 2020.
4. See 'Next generation professional' at <http://reports.devex.com/1028401/>.
5. Ibid.
6. Ibid.

ANNEX 1

WASH indicators within the humanitarian, transition, and post-emergency phases

These tables are based on information from the *UNHCR WASH Manual*, which is one of the first to reflect on the three phases of WASH (Harvey et al., 2020: 6–7). They have been expanded based on information gathered by Save the Children WASH field staff. Save the Children is constantly updating this information; it therefore remains a work in progress and continues to be developed as more is learned about WASH across the humanitarian–development divide.

Indicators are divided into three main sections: WASH in communities, WASH in healthcare facilities, and WASH in educational facilities. Each of these three sections are further divided into separate considerations around water, sanitation, and hygiene.

WASH in communities

Water

List of activities: emergency, transition, and post-emergency phases

Time period	Emergency phase Short term: 0–6 months	Transition phase Medium term: 6 months – 2 years	Post-emergency/ protracted phase Long term: 2–20 years+
Water supply	**Target 7.5–15 l/p/d**	**Target 15–20 l/p/d**	**Target 20+ l/p/d**
	Water trucking	Emergency surface water treatment plant (EmWat)	Borehole source (D304, D305)[1]
	Emergency elevated tank (D306, D307, D308)[1]	Jetwells	Surface source treatment
	Emergency tapstands (D300)	Temporary piped water network using Oxfam tanks, polyethylene (PE) pipes, and tapstands	Elevated water tower (D309, D310)[1]
	Bottled water		Pipe network
	Aquatabs/purifier of water/high test hypochlorite/chlorine[2]	Extension of existing water network	Tapstands (D301)[1]
			Tapstation
	Bucket chlorination point	Borehole source (D304, D305)[1]	Handpump (D302)[1]
			Rainwater harvesting (tank, pond, runoff)

(Continued)

Continued

Time period	Emergency phase Short term: 0–6 months	Transition phase Medium term: 6 months – 2 years	Post-emergency/ protracted phase Long term: 2–20 years+
	Water collection/storage kit distribution	Surface source treatment	Solar power or other renewable source of energy
	Emergency surface water treatment plant (EmWat)	Elevated water tower (D309, D310)[1]	Apartment plumbing upgrades
	Water tank disinfection	Pipe network	Cash/vouchers
		Tapstands (D301)[1]	Spring water source protection
		Handpump (D302)[1]	
		Rainwater harvesting	
		Chlorine production and market sale	
		Household water treatment kits (solar disinfection (SODIS), ceramic water filter, sand filter)	
		Cash/vouchers	
		Spring water source protection	
Water management	Formation of water management committees	Refresher training of water management committees	Integrated water resource management and water governance
	Training of water management committees	Capacity building of water management institutions	Selection and training of HPMs
	Provision of water management kits	Provision of water management kits	
	Capacity building of water management institutions	Capacity building of water vendors	
		Selection and training of handpump mechanics (HPMs)	
		Equipping HPMs with toolkits	
Water investigation	Post-distribution monitoring (PDM)	PDM	PDM
	Baseline/intermediate/ end-line survey	Baseline/intermediate/ end-line survey	Baseline/intermediate/ end-line survey
	Sanitary survey	Sanitary survey	Sanitary survey

[1] Design included in UNHCR (n.d.).
[2] Item specification in UNHCR (2016).

Monitoring: indicators, frequency, and means of verification

Indicator		Emergency target	Post-emergency target	Means of verification
Water quantity	Average # litres of potable water available per person per day	≥ 15	≥ 20	Monthly report card
				Construction/ rehabilitation report
	Average # litres of potable water available per person per day of potable water collected at household level	≥ 15	≥ 20	Annual knowledge, attitudes, and practices (KAP)
				Water point attendance surveys
	% of households with at least 10 litres/ person potable water storage capacity	≥ 70%	≥ 80%	Annual KAP and post-distribution monitoring (PDM) surveys
Water access	Maximum distance from household to potable water collection point	≤ 500m	≤ 200m	Mapping
				Annual KAP survey
	Number of persons per handpump/spring[1]	≤ 500	≤ 250	Monthly report card
				Water point attendance survey
	Number of persons per water tap[2]	≤ 250	≤ 100	Monthly report card
				Water point attendance survey
	Maximum time for collecting water (time to go, queue at water point, and come back home)	≤ 30 min	≤ 30 min	KAP and water point attendance surveys
	Number of field group discussions (FGDs) for safe position or confirm the position for water point (if already exists)	≥ 1 per group	≥ 1 per group	FGDs segregated by gender and age
				Children and people living with disabilities (PLWD) should be consulted in separate FGDs[3]

(Continued)

Continued

Indicator		Emergency target	Post-emergency target	Means of verification
	% of women declaring the water point safe for their use	100%	100%	KAP survey
	% of children declaring the water point safe for their use	100%	100%	KAP survey
	Number of child-friendly taps per water collection point	≥ 1	≥ 1	Construction report
	% of tapstands segregated by gender where culturally relevant	100%	100%	Construction report
	% of water points with no PLWD accessible path[4]	100%	100%	Construction report Monthly visit
	% of water points with PLWD accessible path[5]	80%	90%	Construction report Monthly visit
	% of users satisfied with quality and quantity of kit items received	≥ 90%	≥ 90%	PDM survey
Water quality	% of households consuming safe drinking water	≥ 70%	≥ 95%	Annual KAP survey
	% water quality tests at non-chlorinated water collection locations with 0 colony-forming units (CFUs)/100 ml	≥ 95%	≥ 95%	Monthly report card
	% of water quality tests at chlorinated collection locations with correct free residual chlorine (FRC) results ($0.2 \leq FRC \leq 0.5$ for PH ≤ 8 and $0.5 \leq FRC \leq 1$ for $8 \leq$ PH) and turbidity < 5 nephelometric turbidity units (NTU)	≥ 95%	≥ 95%	Monthly report card

(Continued)

Continued

Indicator		Emergency target	Post-emergency target	Means of verification
	% of water source located at more than 50 m from pollution sources and aquifer located at least 1.5 m below pollution sources (pit latrines, landfill, graveyard)	100%	100%	Construction report Direct observation
	For non-chemical household water treatment kits distributed: % water quality tests at household collection locations with 0 CFUs/100 ml	$\geq$ 95%	$\geq$ 95%	Monthly households visit report
	For chemical household water treatment kits distributed: % water quality tests at household collection locations with correct FRC results ($0.2 \leq$ FRC ≤ 0.5 for PH ≤ 8 and $0.5 \leq$ FRC ≤ 1 for $8 \leq$ PH) and turbidity < 5 NTU[6]	$\geq$ 95%	$\geq$ 95%	Monthly households visit report
	% of water samples analysed at water collection locations in line with national water quality standard (if absent, refer to WHO chemical standard for water quality)	100%	100%	Initial and yearly water quality analysis report
Water management	Number of water management committees newly trained/refreshed per water facility	≥ 1	≥ 1	Training report
	Number of water management kits donated per committee	1	1	Certificate donation
	% of trained water management committees that are active	100%	100%	Monthly meeting with committees

(Continued)

Continued

Indicator		Emergency target	Post-emergency target	Means of verification
	% of water facilities maintained, functional, and clean	100%	100%	Direct observation
	% of female members of water management committees	≥ 50%	≥ 50%	Training attendance list
	% of female members of water management committees that are active	100%	100%	Monthly meeting with committees

[1] 500 persons per hand pump (based on a flow rate of 17 litres/minute), 400 persons per open well (based on a flow rate of 12.5 litres/minute), Sphere standard.

[2] 250 persons per tap (based on a flow rate of 7.5 litres/minute), sphere standard.

[3] Generally, a minimum of five groups should be considered (men, women, boys, girls, and people living with disabilities (PLWD)). Additional groups could be added based on specific contexts (marginalized ethnic groups, groups affected by particular health/social conditions, etc.).

[4] This means that persons with limited ambulation capacity, such as pregnant women, elderly people, and small children, are able to find an accessible path, with steps lower than 15cm or with a slope lower than 10 per cent.

[5] Accessible by persons using wheelchairs, with a slope lower than 8 per cent.

[6] Minimum target at water collection point should be 0.5 mg/L FRC in general, and 1 mg/L FRC during an outbreak.

Sanitation

List of activities: emergency, transition, and post-emergency phases

Time period	Emergency phase Short term: 0–6 months	Transition phase Medium term: 6 months – 2 years	Post-emergency/ protracted phase Long term: 2–20 years+
Excreta management facilities	**Target: 1:50 (communal)**	**Target: 1:20 (shared family)**	**Target: 1:5 or 1 per household**
	Trench toilets (D400, D401)[1]	Increase toilet coverage by commencing household toilet programme, initially with 1 toilet shared between 4 families (1:20) and improving to 1 per household as resources permit	Basic pit toilet dome slab (D402, D403)[1]
	Chemical toilets		Urine diversion (UD) device toilet (D406)[1]
	Elevated/lined desludgeable toilets (D405)[1]		Pour-flush toilet (D404)[1]
	Simple pit toilets		Apartment plumbing upgrades
	Plastic toilet slab[2]	Cash for work	Sewer network/septic tanks
	Plastic sheeting (03153)[2]	**Target 1:20 (communal)**	Wastewater treatment plant
	Potties for children's usage	Semi-durable toilets (wooden/metallic superstructure)	

Continued

Time period	Emergency phase Short term: 0–6 months	Transition phase Medium term: 6 months – 2 years	Post-emergency/ protracted phase Long term: 2–20 years+
	Toilet blocks accessible for people living with disabilities (PLWD) Toilet blocks designed with and for children Toilet blocks segregated by gender	Toilet containers Ventilated improved pit (VIP) toilets	VIP toilets
Bath shelters	**1:50 (communal)** Bath/shower blocks (D700)[1] Bath/shower blocks accessible for PLWD Bath/shower blocks designed with and for children Plastic sheeting (03153)[2] Drainage	**1:20 (shared family)** Increase bath/shower coverage (1 per 4 families) Encourage families to build their own facilities Cash for work **Target 1:20 (communal)** Semi-durable showers (wooden/metallic superstructure) Shower containers	**1:5 or 1 per household** Household bath/shower cubicle Encourage families to build their own facilities
Sanitation facilities management	Training of latrines/showers management committee Provision of latrines/showers management kits Capacity building of local bodies Latrine-digging kits[2] Daily cleaning/maintenance	Cash/vouchers Desludging	Cash/vouchers Desludging/septage treatment Promotion of participatory hygiene and sanitation transformation (PHAST) approach Community training on community-led total sanitation (CLTS) approach
Solid waste management	Rubbish bins (stockpile) Collection services/incentive workers Waste segregation Rubbish pits Clean-up campaigns	Transition to long-term cost-effective community-managed or household-managed solutions Clean-up campaigns Household rubbish pits	Transfer/landfill (D500)[1] Household rubbish pits Recycling and reuse Clean-up campaigns Cash/vouchers

(Continued)

Continued

Time period	Emergency phase Short term: 0–6 months	Transition phase Medium term: 6 months – 2 years	Post-emergency/ protracted phase Long term: 2–20 years+
	Capacity building of local institutions	Capacity building of local institutions	
	Waste safe disposal		
Vector control	Indoor residual spraying[2]	Transition to long-term cost-effective community-managed solutions	Indoor residual spraying[2]
	Treat pit toilets with chlorine or insecticide to kill fly larvae		Rodent control
		Drainage	Disaster risk reduction (DRR) in urban plan
	Pit cover for organic solid waste	Cash for work	
	Impregnated mosquito net distribution	Capacity building of local bodies	
		Cash/vouchers	
	Capacity building of local bodies	Cleaning of bushes	
		Awareness raising to the affected/at risk population	
Laundry facilities	See hygiene kit in hygiene promotion section	Public laundry stands	Public laundry/dryer machines in urban settings
		Cash for work	
			Cash/vouchers

[1] Design included in UNHCR (n.d.).
[2] Item specification in UNHCR (2016).

Monitoring: indicators, frequency, and means of verification

Indicator		Emergency target	Post-emergency target	Means of verification
Excreta management/ bath shelters	Number of persons per functional toilet/latrine/ shower	≤ 50	≤ 20[6]	Monthly report card
	% of households with household toilet/latrine/ shower	–	≥ 85%	Annual knowledge, attitudes, and practices (KAP) survey
	% of households reporting defecating in a toilet/bathing in a bath shelter	≥ 60%	≥ 85%	Annual KAP survey

(Continued)

Continued

Indicator	Emergency target	Post-emergency target	Means of verification
% of toilets/bath blocks at less than 50 m from dwellings	100%	100%	Construction report
% of public adult sanitation facilities segregated by gender (showers/toilets/ handwashing stands)	100%	100%	Construction report
% of public sanitation facilities labelled with pictogram for gender and type of user (patients/staff/children/ people living with disabilities (PLWD))	100%	100%	Construction report Monthly visit
% of public sanitation blocks constructed with at least 1 PLWD-friendly toilet/shower	100%	100%	Construction report
% of sanitation facilities designed with and for children	% of children aged 4–7 years	% of children aged 4–7 years	Construction report
Number of field group discussions (FGDs) for safe position or confirm the position for toilet/ shower (if already exists)	≥ 1 per group	≥ 1 per group	FGDs segregated by gender and age Children and PLWD should be consulted in separate FGDs
% of women declaring the toilet/shower safe for their use	100%	100%	KAP survey
Number of properly fenced and protected toilets/bath shelters	100%	100%	Construction report
Number of public toilets/bath shelters with proper lighting	100%	100%	Construction report
% of children declaring the toilet/shower safe for their use	100%	100%	KAP survey
% of female-use toilets supposed to be used by menstruating-age females with appropriate menstrual hygiene mana- gement (MHM) facility	100%	100%	Construction report

(Continued)

Continued

Indicator		Emergency target	Post-emergency target	Means of verification
	% of females satisfied with MHM facility provided	95%	95%	KAP survey
Sanitation facilities management	Number of sanitation management committees newly trained/refreshed per sanitation (toilet/shower) block	1	1	Training report
	Number of management kits donated per sanitation management committee	1	1	Certificate donation
	% of trained sanitation management committees that are active	100%	100%	Monthly meeting with committees
	% of sanitation facilities that are functional, safe (internal lock and privacy guaranteed), and clean	100%	100%	Final KAP survey Direct observation
	% of active female members of latrine/ shower management committees	≥ 50%	≥ 50%	Training attendance list and interviews
Solid waste	% of households with access to solid waste disposal facility	≥ 70%	≥ 90%	Annual KAP survey
	% of waste generation points where waste is correctly segregated and collected	100%	100%	Monthly observation
	% of waste collection points where waste is correctly segregated and collected	100%	100%	Monthly observation
	% of waste collection containers correctly managed/disposed, if onsite waste management exists	100%	100%	Monthly observation
	% of users satisfied with the service provided	95%	95%	Final KAP survey
Vector control	% of users satisfied with the service provided	95%	95%	Final KAP survey

(Continued)

Continued

Indicator		Emergency target	Post-emergency target	Means of verification
Laundry facility	% of users satisfied with the service provided	95%	95%	Final KAP survey
	Number of persons per tap/stand	≤ 500	≤ 500	List of beneficiaries
	% of laundry facilities with available water	100%	100%	Monthly observation

Hygiene

List of activities: emergency, transition, and post-emergency phases

Time period	Emergency phase Short term: 0–6 months	Transition phase Medium term: 6 months – 2 years	Post-emergency/ protracted phase Long term: 2–20 years+
Handwashing	**Target: 1 handwash device per toilet block** Emergency handwash container 50 litre with tap and stand[2] Soak pit for wastewater Soap[2] Daily refilling/ operations and maintenance Cleaning of handwashing container daily before refilling	**At communal level** Durable/semi-durable handwash facility Soap[2] Daily refilling/operation and maintenance **At family level** Increase handwashing promotion at household level and ensure each shared family toilet is equipped with appropriate handwashing device	**Target: 1 handwash device per household** 2 litre container[2] Washbasin/sink Promotion of locally made handwashing facilities (e.g. Tippy taps)
Hygiene promotion	**1:500 hygiene promoters** Information, education, and communication (IEC) materials (water, sanitation, hygiene, cholera, haemorrhagic fever virus (HFV), etc.)[2] Hygiene kit[2] Baby kit[2] Dignity kit[2] Mass campaign (theatre, radio broadcasting)	**1:500 hygiene promoters** IEC materials (water, sanitation, hygiene, cholera, HFV, etc.)[2] Door-by-door promotion Participatory hygiene and sanitation transformation (PHAST), child hygiene and sanitation training (CHAST), and clean household approach (CHP) methods Cash/vouchers	**1:1,000 hygiene promoters** IEC materials (water, sanitation, hygiene, cholera, HFV, etc.)[2] Refresher training for government structures and handover

(Continued)

Continued

Time period	Emergency phase Short term: 0–6 months	Transition phase Medium term: 6 months – 2 years	Post-emergency/ protracted phase Long term: 2–20 years+
	Capacity building of relevant bodies	Mass campaign/ community hygiene sessions	
	Establishment, training, and incentives for hygiene promoters	Training of government-established structures (vapour heat treatments, community health volunteers, public health assistants, etc.)	
	Disinfection of households for cholera/ HFV cases		
	Community engagement and participation		
	Demonstration of good hygiene practices		

[1] Design included in UNHCR (n.d.).
[2] Item specification in UNHCR (2016).

Monitoring: indicators, frequency, and means of verification

Indicator		Emergency target	Post-emergency target	Means of verification
Handwashing	% of toilet blocks with functional handwashing facility and at less than 5 m	100%	100%	Construction report Monthly visit
	Number of toilets per handwashing tap	8	1	Construction report
	% of handwashing facilities with available water	$\geq 70\%$	$\geq 90\%$	Final knowledge, attitudes, and practices (KAP) survey
	% of handwashing facilities with available soap/ashes	$\geq 70\%$	$\geq 90\%$	Final KAP survey
Hygiene promotion	Number of persons per hygiene promoter	≤ 500	$\leq 1{,}000$	Monthly report card
	% of female hygiene promoters	$\geq 50\%$	$\geq 50\%$	Training attendance list
	% of households with access to soap	$\geq 70\%$	$\geq 90\%$	Annual KAP survey
	% of households knowing at least 3 out of 5 handwashing critical times	$\geq 70\%$	$\geq 90\%$	Final KAP survey

(Continued)

Continued

Indicator		Emergency target	Post-emergency target	Means of verification
	% of households drinking safe water	≥ 70%	≥ 90%	Final KAP survey
	% of households storing their drinking water safely in clean and covered containers	≥ 70%	≥ 90%	Final KAP survey
	% of households using functioning hygienic toilets	≥ 70%	≥ 90%	Final KAP survey
	% of households knowing at least 3 methods to protect themselves from diarrhoea/cholera/haemorrhagic fever virus (HFV)	≥ 70%	≥ 90%	Final KAP survey
	% of households knowing of at least 2 effective vector control measures	≥ 70%	≥ 90%	Final KAP survey
	% of households with absence of solid waste inside and around their dwelling	≥ 70%	≥ 90%	Final KAP survey
	% of households with absence of open defecation around their dwelling	≥ 70%	≥ 90%	Final KAP survey
	% of households using bed impregnated mosquito nets	≥ 70%	≥ 90%	Final KAP survey
	% of users satisfied with quality and quantity of kit items received	≥ 90%	≥ 90%	Post-distribution monitoring (PDM)
	% of households aware of complaint and feedback mechanism	≥ 90%	≥ 90%	Final KAP survey

[1] To maintain health, dignity and well-being, at least 450 g of soap should be distributed per person per month: 250 g is for personal hygiene and 200 g for laundry and other washing purposes.

WASH in healthcare facilities

Water

List of activities: emergency, transition, and post-emergency phases

Time period	Emergency phase Short term: 0–6 months	Transition phase Medium term: 6 months – 2 years	Post-emergency/ protracted phase Long term: 2–20 years+
Water supply	Water trucking

Emergency elevated tank (D306, D307, D308)[1] | Emergency surface water treatment plant (EmWat)

Jetwells/shallow wells | Borehole source (D304, D305)[1]

Surface source and treatment |

(Continued)

Continued

Time period	Emergency phase Short term: 0–6 months	Transition phase Medium term: 6 months – 2 years	Post-emergency/ protracted phase Long term: 2–20 years+
	Emergency tapstand (D300)	Temporary piped water network using Oxfam tanks, polyethylene (PE) pipes, and tapstands	Elevated water tower (D309, D310)[1]
	Bottled water		Pipe network
	Aquatabs/purifier of water/high test hypochlorite/chlorine[2]	Extension of existing water network	Tapstand (D301)[1]
			Handpump (D302)[1]
	Bucket chlorination point	Borehole source (D304, D305)[1]	Rainwater harvesting (tank, pond, runoff)
	Water collection/storage kit distribution	Surface source and treatment	Solar power or other renewable source of energy
		Elevated water tower (D309, D310)[1]	Plumbing upgrades
	Emergency surface water treatment plant (EmWat)/rapid testing kit	Pipe network	Cash/vouchers
	Water tank disinfection	Tapstand (D301)[1]	
		Handpump (D302)[1]	
	Water tank provision/bucket/drums	Rainwater harvesting (tank, pond, runoff)	
	Distribution of water management kits to patients (cholera, haemorrhagic fever virus (HFV), severe acute malnutrition)	Protection of hand-dug wells	
		Domestic filters	
		Distribution of water management kits to patients (cholera, HFV, severe acute malnutrition)	
	Rehabilitation of existing water systems	Cash/vouchers	
Water management	Training of administrative staff on water management	Training of administrative staff on water management	Integrated water resource management
			Refresher training and handover
	Provision of water management kits	Capacity building of water management institutions	
	Capacity building of water management institutions	Provision of water management kits	
		Refresher training and handover	

(Continued)

Continued

Time period	Emergency phase Short term: 0–6 months	Transition phase Medium term: 6 months – 2 years	Post-emergency/ protracted phase Long term: 2–20 years+
Water investigation	Post-distribution monitoring (PDM) Baseline/ intermediate/end-line survey Sanitary survey	PDM Baseline/intermediate/ end-line survey Sanitary survey Hydrogeological/ geophysical survey	PDM Baseline/intermediate/ end-line survey Sanitary survey Hydrogeological/ geophysical survey

Monitoring: indicators, frequency, and means of verification

Indicator		Target	Means of verification
Water quantity	Litres of potable water available per outpatient per day	10	Construction report Direct observation
	Litres of potable water available per inpatient/bed per day	50	
	Litres of water available per intervention, operating theatre or maternity unit	100	
	Litres of potable water available per consultation depending on waiting time – dry or supplementary feeding centre	0.5–5	
	Litres of potable water available per patient per day – therapeutic treatment centre	60	
	Litres of potable water available per patient per day – cholera treatment centre	60	
	Litres of potable water available per patient per day – Ebola treatment centre	300	
	Litres of potable water available per caregiver per day	15	
Water quality	% of water quality tests at chlorinated collection locations with correct free residual chlorine (FRC) results ($0.2 \leq$ FRC ≤ 0.5 for PH ≤ 8 and $0.5 \leq$ FRC ≤ 1 for $8 \leq$ PH) and turbidity < 5 NTU	$\geq 95\%$	Monthly report card
	% of water quality tests at non-chlorinated water collection locations with 0 colony-forming units (CFUs)/100ml	$\geq 95\%$	Monthly report card
	% of water source located at more than 50 m from pollution sources and aquifer located at least 1.5 m below pollution sources (pit latrines, landfill, graveyard)	100%	Construction report Direct observation
	% of water samples analysed at water collection locations in line with national standards or WHO chemical standard for water quality	100%	Initial water quality analysis report

(Continued)

Continued

Indicator		Target	Means of verification
	% of drinking water containers that are clean, with a lid, and properly labelled (also in local language and pictograms)	100%	Monthly visit
Water access	Number of days the water storage capacity allows the facility to meet their needs	2	Construction report
			Direct observation
	Maximum distance from care point to potable water collection point	≤ 500 m	Construction report
	Number of persons per usable water tap	≤ 250	Size of healthcare facility
			Monthly report card
			Water point attendance survey
Water management	Number of administrative staff trained for water management	≥ 2	Training report
	Number of water management kits donated per healthcare facility	1	Donation certificate
	% of trained administrative staff for water management who are active	100%	Monthly meeting
	% of female administrative staff trained for water management	≥ 50%	Training attendance list and interviews
	% of water facilities maintained, functional, and clean	100%	Monthly observation

Sanitation

List of activities: emergency, transition, and post-emergency phases

Time period	Emergency phase Short term: 0–6 months	Transition phase Medium term: 6 months – 2 years	Post-emergency/ protracted phase Long term: 2–20 years+
Excreta management facilities	Chemical toilets	Semi-durable toilets (wooden/metallic superstructure)	Basic pit toilet dome slab (D402, D403)[1]
	Basic pit toilet with plastic toilet slab[2]		Pour-flush toilet (D404)[1]
	Plastic sheeting (03153)[2]	Toilet containers	
		Cash for work	Plumbing upgrades
	Toilet blocks accessible for people living with disabilities (PLWD)	Elevated desludgeable toilets (D405)[1]	Sewer network
	Toilet blocks designed with and for children	Flush/pour-flush toilet to sewer connection	Wastewater treatment plant
	Potty/bucket	Flush/pour-flush toilet to tank or pit	Desludgeable toilets/ septic tanks

(Continued)

Continued

Time period	Emergency phase Short term: 0–6 months	Transition phase Medium term: 6 months – 2 years	Post-emergency/ protracted phase Long term: 2–20 years+
Bath shelters	Bath/shower blocks Bath/shower blocks accessible for PLWD Bath/shower blocks designed with and for children Plastic sheeting Drainage	Semi-durable showers (wooden/metallic superstructure) Shower containers Cash for work Plastic sheeting (03153)[2] Drainage	Durable bath/shower blocks Bath/shower blocks (D700)[1] Bath/shower blocks accessible for PLWD Bath/shower blocks designed with and for children
Sanitation facilities management	Training of administrative staff /hygienist on latrines/ showers management Provision of latrines/ shower management kits Capacity building of local institutions Daily cleaning/maintenance	Cash/vouchers Desludging Disinfecting and decommissioning	Cash/vouchers Desludging/septage treatment Disinfecting and decommissioning
Solid waste management	Rubbish bins/refuse bags segregated by type (non-infectious/infectious/sharps) Emergency incinerator Collection services/ incentive workers Rubbish pits Organic waste pits Capacity building of local bodies/hygienist and waste attendants	Transition to long-term cost-effective solutions Placenta/needle/ashes pits Double chamber incinerator Capacity building of local bodies	Transfer/landfill (D500)[1] Recycling and reuse Cash/vouchers
Vector control	Indoor residual spraying[2] Impregnated mosquito net distribution Capacity building of local bodies Pit cover to prevent access of flies into the pit Drainage for waste water Bush cleaning	Transition to long-term cost-effective community-managed solutions Drainage Mosquito screens for doors and windows Cash for work Capacity building of local bodies Cash/vouchers	Indoor residual spraying[2] Rodent control Disaster risk reduction (DRR) in urban plan

(Continued)

Continued

Time period	Emergency phase Short term: 0–6 months	Transition phase Medium term: 6 months – 2 years	Post-emergency/ protracted phase Long term: 2–20 years+
Laundry facilities	See hygiene kit in hygiene section	Public laundry stands Cash for work	Public laundry/dryer machines in urban settings Cash/vouchers

[1] Design included in UNHCR (n.d.).
[2] Item specification in UNHCR (2016).

Monitoring: indicators, frequency, and means of verification

Indicators		Emergency target	Post-emergency target	Means of verification
Excreta management/ bath shelters	Number of persons per functional toilet in outpatient facilities	≤ 50	≤ 20	Construction report
	Number of patients/beds per functional toilet in inpatient facilities	≤ 20	≤ 10	Construction report
	Number of patients/beds per functional showers in inpatient facilities	≤ 50	≤ 40	Construction report
	% of sanitation facilities at less than 50 m from beds and care points	100%	100%	Construction report
	% of sanitation facilities adequately lit, including at night	100%	100%	Construction report
	% of adult sanitation facilities (showers/toilets/ handwashing stands) segregated by gender and user as patients/staff	100%	100%	Construction report
	% of sanitation facilities labelled with pictogram for gender and type of user (patients/staff/ children/people living with disabilities (PLWD))	100%	100%	Construction report Monthly visit
	% of sanitation facilities designed with and for children (where relevant)	% of average hospitalized children aged 4–7 years	% of average hospitalized children aged 4–7 years	Construction report
	Number of sanitation facilities designed with and for PLWD	1 per 250 persons	1 per 250 persons	Construction report

(Continued)

Continued

Indicators		Emergency target	Post-emergency target	Means of verification
	Number of female field group discussions (FGDs) for safe position or confirm the position for toilet/shower (if already exists)	≥ 1	≥ 1	FGDs segregated by gender and age
				Children and PLWD should be consulted as well in separate FGDs
	% of women declaring the toilet/ shower safe for their use	100%	100%	Knowledge, attitudes, and practices (KAP) survey
	% of children declaring the toilet/ shower safe for their use	100%	100%	KAP survey
	% of female-use toilets with appropriate menstrual hygiene management (MHM) facility	100%	100%	Construction report
	% of female satisfied with MHM facility provided	95%	95%	KAP survey
Sanitation facilities management	Number of administrative staff trained for sanitation management	≥ 2	≥ 2	Training report
	Number of sanitation management kits donated per sanitation (toilet/shower) block	1	1	Donation certificate
	% of trained administrative staff for sanitation facilities management who are active	100%	100%	Monthly meeting
	% of female administrative staff trained for sanitation facilities management	≥ 50%	≥ 50%	Training attendance list and interviews
	% of sanitation facilities that are functional and clean	100%	100%	Cleaning sheet
				Direct observation
Solid waste	% of waste generation points where waste is correctly segregated and collected	100%	100%	Monthly observation
	% of waste collection points where waste is correctly segregated and collected	100%	100%	Monthly observation

(Continued)

Continued

Indicators		Emergency target	Post-emergency target	Means of verification
	% of waste collection containers correctly managed, if onsite waste management exists	100%	100%	Monthly observation
	% of trained staff using PPE while handling waste (collection/management)	100%	100%	Monthly observation
	% of waste treatment and disposal points	100%	100%	Monthly observation
	% of healthcare facility spaces free from trash	100%	100%	Monthly observation
Vector control	% of healthcare facility spaces free from stagnant water	95%	95%	Monthly observation
	% of beds with impregnated mosquito net	100%	100%	Monthly observation
	% of windows and external doors with mosquito screen	100%	100%	Monthly observation
Laundry facility	% of users satisfied with the service provided	95%	95%	Final KAP survey
	Number of persons per tap/stand	≤500	≤ 500	Healthcare facility size
				List of beneficiaries
	% of laundry facilities with available chlorinated water and soap	100%	100%	Monthly observation

Hygiene

List of activities: emergency, transition, and post-emergency phases

Time period	Emergency phase Short term: 0-6 months	Transition phase Medium term: 6 months – 2 years	Post-emergency/ protracted phase Long term: 2–20 years+
Handwashing	**Target: 1 handwash device per toilet block and per point of care**	**Target: 1 handwash device per toilet block and per point of care**	**Target: 1 handwash device per toilet block and per point of care**
	Emergency handwashing container 50 litre with tap and stand[2]	Durable/semi-durable handwashing facility	Washbasin/sink
		Soap[2]	Soap[2]
	Soap[2]	Chlorinated water (0.05% solution)	Chlorinated water (0.05% solution)
	Chlorinated water (0.05% solution)	Alcohol-based hand rub posts	Alcohol-based hand rub posts

(Continued)

Continued

Time period	Emergency phase Short term: 0-6 months	Transition phase Medium term: 6 months – 2 years	Post-emergency/ protracted phase Long term: 2–20 years+
	Alcohol-based hand rub posts	Daily refilling/ maintenance	Daily refilling/ maintenance
	Daily refilling/ maintenance	Rehabilitation of existing sinks	
	Rehabilitation of existing sinks		
Hygiene promotion	Information, education, and communication (IEC) materials (water, sanitation, hygiene, cholera, haemorrhagic fever virus (HFV), etc.)[2]	IEC materials (water, sanitation, hygiene, cholera, HFV, etc.)[2]	IEC materials (water, sanitation, hygiene, cholera, HFV, etc.)[2]
	Hygiene kit/baby kit/ dignity kit[2] distribution to patients (cholera/ HFV/SAM/women's cases)	Hygiene kit/baby kit/dignity kit[2] distribution to patients (cholera/HFV/ SAM/women's cases)	
	Mass campaign (theatre, radio broadcasting) about water, sanitation, hygiene, cholera, HFV	Mass campaign (theatre, radio broadcasting) about water, sanitation, hygiene, cholera, HFV	
	Training and incentives for hygiene promoters	Training and incentives for hygiene promoters	
	Training session to patients and caregivers (water, sanitation, hygiene, HFV)	Training sessions to patients and caregivers (water, sanitation, hygiene, cholera, HFV)	
	Demonstration of good hygiene practices	Training of healthcare workers on WASH promotion	
		Demonstration of good hygiene practices	
Hygiene procedures and capacity building	Infection, prevention, and control (IPC) training for health workers and cleaners	Clean clinic approach training for health workers and cleaners	BASICS (bold action to stop infections in clinical settings)
	Cleaning kit distribution	Cleaning kit distribution	
	Capacity building of relevant bodies	Capacity building of relevant bodies	
	Disinfection of households for cholera/ HFV cases		

Monitoring: indicators, frequency, and means of verification

Indicator		Target	Means of verification
Handwashing	% of toilets block with functional handwashing facility and at less than 5 m	100%	Construction report Monthly visit
	Number of toilets per handwashing tap	8	Construction report
	% of care points with functional handwashing facility at less than 5 m	100%	Construction report Monthly visit
	% of handwashing facilities with available chlorinated water (0.05% solution)	≥ 90%	Final knowledge, attitudes, and practices (KAP) survey Monthly visit
	% of handwashing facilities with available soap	≥ 90%	Final KAP survey Monthly visit
	% of alcohol-based hand rub posts refilled	≥ 90%	Final KAP survey Monthly visit
Hygiene promotion	Number of persons per hygiene promoter	≤ 1000[8]	Monthly report card
	% of female hygiene promoters	≥ 50%	Training attendance list
	% of patients trained in relevant messages (water, sanitation, hygiene/cholera/haemorrhagic fever virus (HFV))	≥ 90%	Daily register of training
	% of households knowing at least 3 out of 5 handwashing critical times	≥ 90%	Final KAP survey
	% of households storing their drinking water safely in clean and covered containers	≥ 90%	Final KAP survey
	% of households knowing at least 2 methods to protect themselves from diarrhoea/cholera	≥ 90%	Final KAP survey
	% of households knowing of at least 2 effective vector control measures	≥ 90%	Final KAP survey
	% of households with absence of solid waste inside and around their dwelling	≥ 90%	Final KAP survey
	% of households with absence of open defecation around their dwelling	≥ 90%	Final KAP survey
	% of users satisfied with quality and quantity of kit items received	≥ 90%	Post-distribution monitoring (PDM)
	% of households aware of complaint and feedback mechanism	≥ 90%	Final KAP survey
Hygiene procedures and capacity building	Total number of chlorinated solution containers properly labelled and closed (0.05%, 0.2%, 0.5%, 2% solutions)	100%	Final KAP survey Monthly observation

(Continued)

Continued

Indicator	Target	Means of verification
% of staff trained in chlorinated solution management knowing correct procedures	100%	Monthly visit
% of cleaners trained in infection, prevention, and control (IPC) and clean clinic approach knowing correct procedures	100%	Monthly visit
% of cleaners using PPE during daily cleaning operations	100%	Final KAP survey Monthly observation
% of healthcare facilities' outdoor spaces with absence of open defecation	100%	Final KAP survey Monthly observation
Record of cleaning visible and signed by cleaners each day	1	Monthly observation

WASH in educational facilities

Water

List of activities: emergency, transition, and post-emergency phases

Time period	Emergency phase Short term: 0–6 months	Transition phase Medium term: 6 months – 2 years	Post-emergency/ protracted phase Long term: 2–20 years+
Water supply	Water trucking Emergency elevated tank (D306, D307, D308)[1] Emergency tapstand (D300) Bottled water Aquatabs/purifier of water/high test hypochlorite/ chlorine[2] Bucket chlorination point Water collection/ storage kit distribution Emergency surface water treatment plant (EmWat)	Emergency surface water treatment plant (EmWat) Jetwells Temporary piped water network using Oxfam tanks, polyethylene (PE) pipes, and tapstands Extension of existing water network Borehole source (D304, D305)[1] Surface source and treatment Elevated water tower (D309, D310)[1] Pipe network	Borehole source (D304, D305)[1] Surface source and treatment Elevated water tower (D309, D310)[1] Pipe network Tapstand (D301)[1] Handpump (D302)[1] Rainwater harvesting (tank, pond, runoff) Solar power or other renewable source of energy Plumbing upgrades Cash/vouchers

(Continued)

Continued

Time period	Emergency phase Short term: 0–6 months	Transition phase Medium term: 6 months – 2 years	Post-emergency/ protracted phase Long term: 2–20 years+
	Water tank disinfection	Tapstand (D301)[1] Handpump (D302)[1]	
	Water tank provision	Rainwater harvesting (tank, pond, runoff)	
	Distribution of water management kits to students	Domestic filters	
		Distribution of water management kits to students	
		Cash/vouchers	
Water management	Training of administrative staff on water management	Training of administrative staff on water management	Integrated water resource management
	Provision of water management kits	Capacity building of water management bodies	
	Capacity building of water management bodies	Provision of water management kits	
Water investigation	Post-distribution monitoring (PDM)	PDM	PDM
	Baseline/ intermediate/end-line survey	Baseline/ intermediate/end-line survey	Baseline/intermediate/ end-line survey
	Sanitary survey	Sanitary survey	Sanitary survey

[1] Design included in UNHCR (n.d.).
[2] Item specification in UNHCR (2016).

Monitoring: indicators, frequency, and means of verification

Indicator		Target	Means of verification
Water quantity	Litres of potable water available per student/ teacher	3	Construction report
	Litres of potable water available per student/ teachers if in dorms	≥ 20	Direct observation
Water quality	% of water quality tests at chlorinated collection locations with correct free residual chlorine (FRC) results ($0.2 \leq FRC \leq 0.5$ for PH ≤ 8 and $0.5 \leq FRC \leq 1$ for $8 \leq$ PH) and turbidity < 5 NTU	$\geq 95\%$	Monthly report card

(Continued)

Continued

Indicator		Target	Means of verification
	% water quality tests at non-chlorinated water collection locations with 0 colony-forming units (CFUs)/100 ml	≥ 95%	Monthly report card
	% of water source located at more than 50 m from pollution sources and aquifer located at least 1.5 m below pollution sources (pit latrines, landfill, graveyard)	100%	Construction report Direct observation
	% of water samples analysed at water collection locations in line with national standard or WHO chemical standard for water quality	100%	Initial water quality analysis report
	% of drinking water containers that are clean, with a lid and properly labelled (also in local language and pictograms)	100%	Monthly visit
Water access	Number of days per month the school had no or insufficient access to water	0	Monthly visit
	Pupils per functional tap	200	Construction report
	% of taps with design appropriate for users' age (child-friendly taps)	100%	Construction report
	Number of drinking water taps that can be used by people living with disabilities (PLWD)	1 per water drinking station	Construction report
Water management	Number of administrative staff trained for water management	≥ 2	Training report
	Number of water management kits donated per education facility	1	Donation certificate
	% of trained administrative staff for water management who are active	100%	Monthly meeting
	% of female administrative staff trained for water management	≥ 50%	Training attendance list and interviews
	% of water facilities maintained, functional, and clean	100%	Monthly observation

Sanitation

List of activities: emergency, transition, and post-emergency phases

Time period	Emergency phase Short term: 0–6 months	Transition phase Medium term: 6 months – 2 years	Post-emergency/ protracted phase Long term: 2–20 years+
Excreta management facilities	Trench toilets (D400, D401)[1] Chemical toilets	Semi-durable toilets (wooden/metallic superstructure)	Basic pit toilet dome slab (D402, D403)[1] Pour-flush toilet (D404)[1]

(Continued)

Continued

Time period	Emergency phase Short term: 0–6 months	Transition phase Medium term: 6 months – 2 years	Post-emergency/ protracted phase Long term: 2–20 years+
	Elevated desludgeable toilets (D405)[1]	Toilet containers	Plumbing upgrades
		Cash for work	Sewer network
	Plastic toilet slab[2]		Wastewater treatment plant
	Plastic sheeting (03153)[2]		
	Toilet blocks accessible for people living with disabilities (PLWD)		
	Toilet blocks designed with and for children		
Bath shelters	Bath/shower blocks (D700)[1]	Semi-durable showers (wooden/metallic superstructure)	Durable bath/shower blocks
	Bath/shower blocks accessible for PLWD	Shower containers	
	Bath/shower blocks designed with and for children	Cash for work	
	Plastic sheeting (03153)[2]		
	Drainage		
Sanitation facilities management	Training of administrative staff on latrines/showers management	Cash/vouchers	Cash/vouchers
		Desludging	Desludging/septage treatment
	Provision of latrines/showers management kits		Child hygiene and sanitation training (CHAST) promotion
	Capacity building of local bodies		
	Daily cleaning/ maintenance		
Solid waste management	Rubbish bins	Transition to long-term cost-effective solutions	Transfer/landfill (D500)[1]
	Collection services/ incentive workers		Recycling and reuse
		Double chamber incinerator	Cash/vouchers
	Rubbish pits		
	Emergency incinerator	Capacity building of local bodies	
	Capacity building of local bodies		

(Continued)

Continued

Time period	Emergency phase Short term: 0–6 months	Transition phase Medium term: 6 months – 2 years	Post-emergency/ protracted phase Long term: 2–20 years+
Vector control	Indoor residual spraying[2] Treat pit toilets with chlorine or insecticide to kill fly larvae Capacity building of local bodies	Transition to long-term cost-effective community-managed solutions Drainage Mosquito screens for doors and windows Cash for work Capacity building of local bodies Cash/vouchers	Indoor residual spraying[2] Rodent control Disaster risk reduction (DRR) in urban plan
Laundry facilities	See hygiene kit in hygiene section	Public laundry stands Cash for work	Public laundry/dryer machines in urban settings Cash/vouchers

[1] Design included in UNHCR (n.d.).
[2] Item specification in UNHCR (2016).

Monitoring: indicators, frequency, and means of verification

Indicators		Emergency target	Post-emergency target	Means of verification
Excreta management/ bath shelters	Number of girls per toilet	≤ 50	≤ 30	Construction report
	Number of boys per toilet	≤ 60	≤ 60	Construction report
	Number of adults per functional toilet	≤ 50	≤ 20	Construction report
	Number of persons per functional toilet in dorms	≤ 50	≤ 20	Construction report
	Number of persons per functional showers in dorms	≤ 50	≤ 40	Construction report
	% of sanitation facilities at less than 50 m from users (classrooms/dorms)	100%	100%	Construction report
	% of sanitation facilities adequately lit, including at night	100%	100%	Construction report
	% of sanitation facilities (showers/ toilets/handwashing stands) segregated by gender and user (students/teachers/children needing child-friendly toilets)	100%	100%	Construction report

(Continued)

Continued

Indicators		Emergency target	Post-emergency target	Means of verification
	% of sanitation facilities labelled with pictogram for gender and type of user (students/teachers/children needing child-friendly toilets/ people living with disabilities (PLWD))	100%	100%	Construction report Monthly visit
	% of sanitation facilities designed with and for children	% of children aged 4–7 years	% of children aged 4–7 years	Construction report
	Number of sanitation facilities designed with and for PLWD	1 per 250 persons	1 per 250 persons	Construction report
	Number of field group discussions (FGDs) for safe position or confirm the position for toilet/ shower (if already exists)	≥ 1 per group	≥ 1 per group	FGDs segregated by gender and age Children and PLWD should be consulted as well in separate FGDs
	% of women declaring the toilet/ shower safe for their use	100%	100%	Knowledge, attitudes, and practices (KAP) survey
	% of children declaring the toilet/ shower safe for their use	100%	100%	KAP survey
	% of female-use (women and teenagers) toilets with appropriate menstrual hygiene management (MHM) facility	100%	100%	Construction report
	% of females (women and teenagers) satisfied with MHM facility provided	95%	95%	KAP survey
Sanitation facilities management	Number of administrative staff trained for sanitation management	≥ 2	≥ 2	Training report
	Number of sanitation management kits donated per sanitation (toilet/shower) block	1	1	Donation certificate

(Continued)

Continued

Indicators		Emergency target	Post-emergency target	Means of verification
	% of trained administrative staff for sanitation facilities management who are active	100%	100%	Monthly meeting
	% of female administrative staff trained for sanitation facilities management	≥ 50%	≥ 50%	Training attendance list and interviews
	% of sanitation facilities that are functional and clean	100%	100%	Cleaning sheet
				Direct observation
Solid waste	% of waste generation points where waste is correctly segregated and collected	100%	100%	Monthly observation
	% of waste collection point where waste is correctly segregated and collected	100%	100%	Monthly observation
	% of waste collection containers correctly managed/ disposed, if onsite waste management exists	100%	100%	Monthly observation
	% of trained staff using PPE while manipulating waste (collection/ management)	100%	100%	Monthly observation
	% of education facility spaces free from trash	100%	100%	Monthly observation
Vector control	% of education facility spaces free from stagnant water	95%	95%	Monthly observation
	% of beds with impregnated mosquito net in dorms	100%	100%	Monthly observation
	% of windows and external doors with mosquito screen	100%	100%	Monthly observation
Laundry facility (in dorms)	% of users satisfied with the service provided	95%	95%	Final KAP survey
	Number of persons per tap/stand	≤ 500	≤ 500	List of beneficiaries
	% of laundry facilities with available water and soap	100%	100%	Monthly observation

Hygiene

List of activities: emergency, transition, and post-emergency phases

Time period	Emergency phase Short term: 0–6 months	Transition phase Medium term: 6 months – 2 years	Post-emergency/ protracted phase Long term: 2–20 years+
Handwashing	**Target: 1 handwash device per toilet block and per point of care**	**Target: 1 handwash device per toilet block and per point of care**	**Target: 1 handwash device per toilet block and per point of care**
	Emergency handwashing container 50 litres with tap and stand[2]	Durable/semi-durable handwashing facility	Washbasin/sink
	Soap[2]	Soap[2]	Soap[2]
	Chlorinated water (0.05% solution)	Chlorinated water (0.05% solution)	Chlorinated water (0.05% solution)
	Alcohol-based hand rub posts	Alcohol-based hand rub posts	Alcohol-based hand rub posts
	Daily refilling/ maintenance	Daily refilling/ maintenance	Daily refilling/ maintenance
Hygiene promotion	Information, education, and communication (IEC) materials (water, sanitation, hygiene, cholera, haemorrhagic fever virus (HFV), etc.)[2]	IEC materials (water, sanitation, hygiene, cholera, HFV, etc.)[2]	IEC materials (water, sanitation, hygiene, cholera, HFV, etc.)[2]
	Hygiene kit/dignity kit[2] distribution to patients (cholera/HFV/SAM/ women's cases)	Hygiene kit/dignity kit[2] distribution to patients (cholera/HFV/SAM/ women's cases)	
	Mass campaign (theatre, radio broadcasting) about water, sanitation, hygiene, cholera, HFV, etc.	Mass campaign (theatre, radio broadcasting) about water, sanitation, hygiene, cholera, HFV	
	Training session to students and teachers (water, sanitation, hygiene, cholera, HFV)	Training session to students and teachers (water, sanitation, hygiene, cholera, HFV)	
	Cleaning campaign by students	Cleaning campaign by students	
		Child-to-child campaign	
Hygiene procedures and capacity building	Cleaning kit distribution	Cleaning kit distribution	Capacity building of relevant bodies
	Capacity building of relevant bodies	Capacity building of relevant bodies	
	Disinfection of schools (cholera/HFV outbreaks)		

[1] Design included in UNHCR (n.d.).
[2] Item specification in UNHCR (2016).

Monitoring: indicators, frequency, and means of verification

Indicator		Target	Means of verification
Handwashing	% of toilets block with functional handwashing facility and at less than 5 m	100%	Construction report
			Monthly visit
	% of child-friendly blocks with child-friendly handwashing taps	100%	Construction report
	% of people living with disabilities (PLWD) toilets with handwashing taps that can be used by PLWD	100%	Construction report
	Number of toilets per handwashing tap	8	Construction report
	% of handwashing facilities with available water	≥ 90%	Final knowledge, attitudes, and practices (KAP) survey
			Monthly visit
	% of handwashing facilities with available soap/ashes	≥ 90%	Final KAP survey
			Monthly visit
Hygiene promotion	% of students and teachers trained in relevant messages	≥ 90%	Register of training
	% of students knowing at least 3 out of 5 handwashing critical times	≥ 90%	Final KAP survey
	% of students storing their drinking water safely in clean and covered containers	≥ 90%	Final KAP survey
	% of students knowing at least 2 methods to protect themselves from diarrhoea/cholera	≥ 90%	Final KAP survey
	% of students knowing of at least 2 effective vector control measures	≥ 90%	Final KAP survey
	% of users satisfied with quality and quantity of kit items received	≥ 90%	Post-distribution monitoring (PDM)
	% of students aware of complaint and feedback mechanism	≥ 90%	Final KAP survey
Hygiene procedures and capacity building	% of cleaners using PPE during daily cleaning operations	100%	Final KAP survey
			Monthly observation

(Continued)

Continued

Indicator	Target	Means of verification
% of education facilities' outdoor spaces with absence of open defecation	100%	Final KAP survey
		Monthly observation
Record of cleaning visible and signed by cleaners each day	1	Monthly observation

ANNEX 2
WASH in non-household settings linked to COVID-19

The table below can be found in an article by Howard et al. (2020) entitled 'COVID-19: urgent actions, critical reflections and future relevance of "WaSH": lessons for the current and future pandemics'. We reproduce it here as a useful guide for adapting WASH programmes to meet additional needs due to a pandemic in non-household settings. The table highlights the unique considerations posed by pandemics and the spread of disease in non-household settings.

Settings	Issues
Healthcare facilities	Separating COVID-19 patients and surges in the number of severe cases, overburden water systems and facility hygiene.
	Deficient healthcare facilities can become epicentres of infection, as with cholera (Mhalu et al., 1984) and Ebola (Faye et al., 2015).
	In many low- and middle-income countries, facilities are chronically under-staffed (WHO, 2006) and resources for cleaning and disinfection are insufficient.
	Only 2% of facilities, in low- and middle-income countries with data, had adequate water, sanitation, hygiene, waste management services and standard precaution items (i.e. PPE) (Cronk and Bartram, 2018).
	WHO and UNICEF (2019) note that 74% of healthcare facilities had at least an improved water source on premises (55% for 'least developed' countries and 51% in sub-Saharan Africa); and 16% had no hygiene service (no water and no sanitation and no handwashing facilities).
	Conventional sanitation facilities require hand-surface contact (door handles, taps, seats, etc.).
Transport	National responses to COVID-19 restrict movement because disease spreads through transportation corridors, as with cholera (Lee and Dodgson, 2000), SARS (Ruan et al., 2005) and influenza (Grais et al., 2020).
	Persons from different households are crowded together in transport and at transport hubs.
	Transport hubs (bus and train stations, shared taxi boarding points, ports and airports) are high-risk locations. They require more frequent hygiene behaviours and enhanced facility cleaning and disinfection during pandemics.

(Continued)

Continued

Settings	Issues
	Pay-to-use facilities discourage desired behaviours and impede frequent hand hygiene.
	Public or shared transport (buses, trains, shared taxis, ferries, aeroplanes) is often over-crowded and hand sanitiser on entry and exit and frequent disinfection are needed.
	Regulating hygiene, regular cleaning and eliminating over-crowding demand assertive action by governments.
	In many countries, migrant labourers have left towns and cities to return [to] their home villages and are exposed to high-risk environments during travel. Facilities in home villages may be insufficient to cope with the increased demand.
Forcibly displaced populations – refugees and internally displaced people	Numbered over 70 million people in 2018 (UNHCR, 2019), more than 60% live in urban host communities rather than camps.
	Most refugees flee to nations that have not met the WASH needs of their citizens.
	Governments anticipate displaced population return to their country of origin, but the average refugee spends 17 years displaced (Behnke et al., 2018).
	Camp settings in emergency (Banner-Shackelford et al., 2020), transitional (Cooper et al., 2021), and protracted (Behnke et al., 2020) phases have deficient environmental health, poor access to hygiene facilities, and close proximity and frequent interaction of households and individuals.
	Sharing and queuing for water sources, toilets, laundry, and bathing facilities are frequent.
	Insufficient water for hand hygiene. For COVID-19 positive households, the burden of water collection may mean health and hygiene suffer.
	Travel for work or returning home can seed continued or second-wave transmission.
Residential care homes for the elderly	Dense populations allow viral spread in a highly vulnerable population.
	Movement of employees in and out of facilities increases transmission risks.
	Ensuring facilities are hygienic and ensuring good hygiene among residents is challenging.
Penal institutions, children's homes, homeless shelters and migrant hostels	Tendency for over-crowding and deficient environmental health (Moffa et al., 2018, 2019; Guo et al., 2019).
	Migrant hostels represent a specific setting of concern as they are often over-crowded with limited WASH facilities; migrants may be indebted as part of arrangements for their employment meaning they must continue to work; and the rights of migrants may be limited.

(Continued)

Continued

Settings	Issues
	Penal institutions and homeless shelters tend to have higher proportions of people with other health problems that may increase susceptibility.
Schools	In 2016, only 69% of schools had at least a basic drinking-water supply (an 'improved water source' with water available at the time of the survey); and 53% had at least a 'basic handwashing facility' (with water and soap available at the time of the survey) (UNICEF and WHO, 2018).
	Compliance with handwashing protocols may be difficult to enforce even where facilities are available.
Workplaces	Workplaces include formal, informal and mobile/itinerant settings and have been the locus of COVID clusters.
	Data on WASH in workplaces are few (Cronk et al., 2015) especially for informal and mobile workers.
	Typical WASH facilities or work practices often require substantive modification to accommodate enhanced hand hygiene and physical distancing.
	Entertainment centres (bars, cafes, restaurants, etc.) are typically crowded and maintenance of hygiene in toilets and provision of sufficient handwashing facilities in toilets may be challenging. Where alcohol is consumed, ensuring hand hygiene behaviours are maintained can be challenging.
Markets	Sufficient handwashing and sanitation facilities in markets are critical and should be supplemented with hand sanitising facilities; cleaning and disinfection should be frequent.
	Pay-to-use facilities may discourage desired behaviours, impede frequent hand hygiene and be insufficiently protective.
	Lessons must be learnt from the 2013–2016 West African Ebola outbreak on special provision of handwashing stations in public places.

Source: Howard et al. (2020). Reproduced under Creative Commons Attribution 4.0 International Licence (CC BY 4.0) <https://creativecommons.org/licenses/by/4.0/>.

ANNEX 3
The Triple Nexus in WASH meeting

The Triple Nexus in WASH meeting took place on 11–12 February 2021 and was organized by the German WASH Network in collaboration with the Global WASH Cluster, Sanitation and Water for All (SWA), UNICEF, and German Humanitarian Assistance (Grieve et al., 2021). This meeting took place after the bulk of this publication was written. We add the meeting speakers here to highlight the ongoing nature of the discussion around WASH and how it bridges the triple nexus.

Name	Title
Key speakers	
Catarina de Albuquerque	Chief Executive Officer, SWA
Gidon Bromberg	Director, EcoPeace Middle East
Francis Bwalya	Permanent Mission of Zambia
Alexandra Campbell-Ferrari	Executive Director, Center for Water Security and Cooperation
Tim Grieve	Independent consultant
Annette Huber-Lee	Senior Scientist, Stockholm Environment Institute
Pit Koehler	Head of Division 'Multilateral Policy on Humanitarian Assistance', German Federal Foreign Office
Peter Mahal	Director General, Ministry of Electricity, Dams, Irrigation and Water Resource of South Sudan
Kelly Ann Naylor	Associate Director of WASH, UNICEF
Monica Ramos	Coordinator, GWC
Perry Rivera	Chief Operating Officer, Manila Water
Michael Talhami	Senior Advisor, Water and Habitat, ICRC
Mara Tignino	Senior Legal Advisor, Geneva Water Hub
Danilo Türk	Lead Political Advisor, Geneva Water Hub (formerly Chair of UN High-Level Panel on Water and Peace and President of Slovenia)
Anna Azaryeva Valente	Team Lead, Fragility and Peacebuilding, UNICEF
Dominick De Waal	Senior Economist, Global Water Practice, World Bank
Key speakers on the SWA building blocks	
Omar El Hattab, Sector Strategy	Senior Advisor Emergencies, WASH Section, UNICEF
Guy Hutton, Financing	Senior Advisor, WASH Section, UNICEF

(Continued)

Continued

Name	Title
Joost Kooijmans, Planning, Monitoring, and Evaluation	Chief Operating Officer, SWA
Monica Ramos, Institutional Arrangements	Coordinator, GWC
Evita Rozenberg and Will Tillett, Capacity Development	IRC and United Purpose
Other speakers	
Marc-André Bünzli	Head Expert Group WASH, Swiss Development Cooperation
Tamarial Abdul Malik	WASH Cluster National Co-Lead, Afghanistan
Thilo Panzerbieter	Chair, German WASH Network

References

A4EP (2021) 'Future course for a Grand Bargain 2.0: time to walk side by side', Alliance for Empowering Partnership <https://resourcecentre.savethechildren.net/node/19011/pdf/a4ep-future-of-gb-statement.pdf>.

Advisory Commission on Rakhine State (2017) *Toward a Peaceful, Fair and Prosperous Future for the People of Rakhine: Final Report of the Advisory Commission on Rakhine State*, Advisory Commission on Rakhine State, Yangon, Myanmar <https://www.rakhinecommission.org/app/uploads/2017/08/FinalReport_Eng.pdf>.

Banner-Shackelford, B., Cronk, R., Behnke, N., Cooper, B., D'Souza, M., Tu, R., Bartram, J., Schweitzer, R. and Jaff, D. (2020) 'Environmental health in forced displacement: a systematic scoping review of the emergency phase', *Science of the Total Environment* 714: 136553.

Bartram, J., Cronk, R., Montgomery, M., Gordon, B., Neira, M., Kelley, E. and Velleman, Y. (2015) 'Lack of toilets and safe water in health-care facilities', *Bulletin of the World Health Organization* 93 (4): 210 <https://doi.org/10.2471/BLT.15.154609>.

Bastable, A. and Russell, L. (2013) *Gap Analysis in Emergency, Water, Sanitation and Hygiene Promotion*, Humanitarian Innovation Fund, Cardiff and London <https://www.alnap.org/help-library/gap-analysis-in-emergency-water-sanitation-and-hygiene-promotion>.

Behnke, N., Cronk, R., Snel, M., Moffa, M., Tu, R., Banner, B., Folz, C., Anderson, D., McIntyre, A., Stowe, E. and Bartram, J. (2018) 'Improving environmental conditions for involuntarily displaced populations: water, sanitation, and hygiene in orphanages, prisons, and refugee and IDP settlements', *Journal of Water Sanitation and Hygiene for Development* 8 (4): 785–91 <https://doi.org/10.2166/washdev.2018.019>.

Behnke, N., Cronk, R., Banner, B., Cooper, B., Tu, R., Heller, L. and Bartram, J. (2020) 'Environmental health conditions in protracted displacement: a systematic scoping review', *Science of the Total Environment* 726: 138234.

Bennett, C., Foley, M. and Pantuliano, S. (2016) *Time to Let Go: A Three-point Proposal to Change the Humanitarian System*, Overseas Development Institute, London <https://www.alnap.org/help-library/time-to-let-go-a-three-point-proposal-to-change-the-humanitarian-system>.

Bill and Melinda Gates Foundation (2020) *COVID-19: A Global Perspective. 2020 Goalkeepers Report*, Bill and Melinda Gates Foundation, Seattle <https://ww2.gatesfoundation.org/goalkeepers/downloads/2020-report/report_letter_en.pdf>.

Blanchet, K., Ramesh, A., Frison, S., Warren, E., Hossain, M., Smith, J., Knight, A., et al. (2017) 'Evidence on public health interventions in humanitarian crises', *The Lancet* 390 (June) <https://doi.org/10.1016/S0140-6736(16)30768-1>.

Brabant, K. Van and Patel, S. (2018) *Localisation in Practice: Emerging Indicators and Practical Recommendations, Global Mentoring Initiative*, Begnins, Switzerland <https://reliefweb.int/report/world/localisation-practice-emerging-indicators-and-practical-recommendations>.

Brown, J., Cavill, S., Cumming, O. and Jeandron, A. (2012) 'Water, sanitation, and hygiene in emergencies: summary review and recommendations for further research', *Waterlines* 31 (1/2): 11–29 <https://doi.org/10.3362/1756-3488.2012.004>.

Cooper, B., Cronk, R., Behnke, N.L., Anthonj, C., Shackelford, B.B., Tu, R. and Bartram, J. (2021) 'Environmental health conditions in the transitional stage of forcible displacement: a systematic scoping review', *Science of the Total Environment* 762: 143136 <https://doi.org/10.1016/j.scitotenv.2020.143136>.

Cronk, R. and Bartram, J. (2018) 'Environmental conditions in health care facilities in low- and middle-income countries: coverage and inequalities', *International Journal of Hygiene and Environmental Health* 221 (3): 409–22.

Cronk, R., Slaymaker, T. and Bartram, J. (2015) 'Monitoring drinking water sanitation and hygiene in non-household settings: priorities for policy and practice', *International Journal of Hygiene and Environmental Health* 218: 694–703 <https://doi.org/10.1016/j.ijheh.2015.03.003>.

Danert, K. and Hutton, G. (2020) 'Shining the spotlight on household investments for water, sanitation and hygiene (WASH): let us talk about HI and the three "T"s', *Journal of Water, Sanitation and Hygiene for Development* 10 (1): 1–4 <https://doi.org/10.2166/washdev.2020.139>.

Devex Editor (2020) 'What does the global development job market look like for 2020?', Devex', March <https://www.devex.com/news/what-does-the-global-development-job-market-look-like-for-2020-96796>.

D'Mello-Guyett, L., Yates, T., Bastable, A., Dahab, M., Deola, C., Dorea, C., Dreibelbis, R., et al. (2018) 'Setting priorities for humanitarian water, sanitation and hygiene research: a meeting report', *Conflict and Health* 12 (22) <https://doi.org/10.1186/s13031-018-0159-8>.

DuBois, M. (2016) 'Don't blur the lines between development and humanitarian work', *Guardian*, 12 May <https://www.theguardian.com/global-development-professionals-network/2016/may/12/dont-blur-the-lines-between-development-and-humanitarian-work>.

DuBois, M. (2020) 'Searching for the nexus: why we're looking in the wrong place', The New Humanitarian, 7 January [online] <https://www.thenewhumanitarian.org/opinion/2020/1/7/triple-nexus-international-aid-Marc-DuBois>.

European Commission (2014) 'Water, hygiene and sanitation (WASH): ECHO factsheet', European Commission, Humanitarian Aid and Civil Protection, Brussels <https://ec.europa.eu/echo/files/aid/countries/factsheets/thematic/wash.pdf>.

Fanning, E. and Fullwood-Thomas, J. (2019) 'The humanitarian–development-peace nexus: what does it mean for multi-mandated organizations?', Oxfam GB, Oxford.

FAO (2019) *Special Report – The 2018 FAO/WFP Agriculture and Food Security Mission to Rakhine State, Myanmar, 2018*, Food and Agriculture Organization of the United Nations, Rome <http://www.fao.org/3/ca5330en/ca5330en.pdf>.

Faye, O., Boëlle, P.-Y., Heleze, E., Faye, O., Loucouber, C., Magassouba, N., Soropogue, B., Keita, S., Gakou, T., Bah, E.H.I., Koivpogui, L., Sal, A.A. and Cauchemez, S. (2015) 'Chains of transmission and control of Ebola virus disease in Conakry, Guinea, in 2014: an observational study', *Lancet Infectious Disease* 15: 320–6 <https://doi.org/10.1016/S1473-3099(14)71075-8>.

Fonseca, C. and Pories, L. (2017) 'Financing WASH: how to increase funds for the sector while reducing inequities: position paper for the Sanitation and Water for All Finance Ministers Meeting', IRC, water.org, Ministry of Foreign Affairs, and Simavi, The Hague <https://www.ircwash.org/resources/financing-wash-how-increase-funds-sector-while-reducing-inequalities-position-paper>.

German WASH Network (2019) *Building Resilient WASH Systems in Fragile Contexts: Event Report*, German WASH Network, Berlin <https://www.washnet.de/wp-content/uploads/2020/07/washnet19_LE-HDN_report_200216_jr.pdf>.

Global Health Cluster and Global WASH Cluster (2020) *Joint Operational Framework: Improving Coordinated and Integrated Multi-sector Cholera Preparedness and Response within Humanitarian Crises*, Global Health Cluster and Global WASH Cluster, Geneva.

Global WASH Cluster (2019) *Delivering Humanitarian WASH at Scale, Anywhere and Any Time: Road Map for 2020–2025*, WASH Cluster, Geneva.

Grais, R.F., Ellis, J.H. and Glass, G.E. (2020) 'Assessing the impact of airline travel on the geographic spread of pandemic influenza', *European Journal of Epidemiology* 18 (11): 1065–72 <https://doi.org/10.1023/A:1026140019146>.

Grieve, T., Rueck, J., Panzerbieter, T., Ramos, M., Bouvet, F., Kooijmans, J. and El Hattab, O. (2021) 'Event report: the Triple Nexus in WASH Humanitarian Development Peace Meeting 11–12 February 2021', German WASH Network.

Grünewald, F., Luff, R., Dehove, E. and Brangeon, S. (2019) *The Capacity of the WASH Sector to Respond to Difficult Humanitarian Situations: An Analysis*, Global WASH Cluster, Geneva <https://www.urd.org/en/project/global-study-on-the-capacity-of-the-wash-sector-to-respond-to-emergencies/>.

Guinote, F.S. (2018) 'A humanitarian–development nexus that works – world', ReliefWeb, 21 June <https://reliefweb.int/report/world/humanitarian-development-nexus-works>.

Guo, W., Cronk, R., Scherer, E., Oommen, R., Brogan, J., Sarr, M.M. and Bartram, J. (2019) 'A systematic review of environmental health conditions in penal institutions', *International Journal of Hygiene and Environmental Health* 222 (5): 790–803 <https://doi.org/10.1016/j.ijheh.2019.05.001>.

Harvey, B., Burt, M., Golay, F. and Schweitzer, R. (2020) *UNHCR WASH Manual: Practical Guidance for Refugee Settings*, UNHCR, Geneva <https://cms. emergency.unhcr.org/documents/11982/38435/UNHCR+WASH+Manual+- +7th+Edition+%28UNHCR%2C+2020%29+%281%29/5d0e7c78-ecb9-4877- bf95-caa290b4add4>.

Howard, G., Bartram, J., Brocklehurst, C., Colford, J., Costa, F., Cunliffe, D., Dreibelbis, R., et al. (2020) 'COVID-19: urgent actions, critical reflections and future relevance of "WaSH": lessons for the current and future pandemics', *Journal of Water and Health* 18 (July): 613–30 <https://doi. org/10.2166/wh.2020.162>.

Huston, A. and Moriarty, P. (2018) 'Understanding the WASH system and its building blocks: building strong WASH systems for the SDGs', IRC, The Hague <https://www.ircwash.org/resources/understanding-wash-system- and-its-building-blocks>.

Hutton, G. (2015) 'Water and sanitation assessment paper: benefits and costs of the water and sanitation targets for the post-2015 development agenda', World Bank, Washington DC.

Hutton, G. and Varughese, M. (2016) *The Costs of Meeting the 2030 Sustainable Development Goal Targets on Drinking Water, Sanitation, and Hygiene*, World Bank, Washington DC <https://doi.org/10.1596/K8543>.

IASC (n.d.) 'The Grand Bargain (official website)', Inter-Agency Standing Committee <https://interagencystandingcommittee.org/grand-bargain>.

ICRC (2015) *Urban Services during Protracted Armed Conflict: A Call for a Better Approach to Assisting Affected People*, International Committee of the Red Cross, Geneva <https://www.icrc.org/sites/default/files/topic/file_plus_ list/4249_urban_services_during_protracted_armed_conflict.pdf>.

ICVA (2017) 'The Grand Bargain explained: an ICVA briefing paper', International Council of Voluntary Agencies, Geneva <https://reliefweb. int/sites/reliefweb.int/files/resources/ICVA_Grand_Bargain_Explained. pdf>.

IOM, NRC, and UNHCR (2015) *Camp Management Toolkit 2015*, International Organization for Migration, Norwegian Refugee Council, and UN Refugee Agency, London <https://www.refworld.org/pdfid/526f6cde4.pdf>.

IRC (2007) *Toward Effective Programming for WASH in Schools: A Manual on Scaling Up Programmes for Water, Sanitation and Hygiene in Schools*, TP Series No. 48, IRC International Water and Sanitation Centre, Delft <https:// www.unicef.org/wash/files/TP_48_WASH_Schools_07.pdf>.

Jama, A.A. and Mourad, K. (2019) 'Water services sustainability: institu- tional arrangements and shared responsibilities', *Sustainability* 11 (3): 916 <https://doi.org/10.3390/su11030916>.

Jiménez, A., Saikia, P., Giné, R., Avello, P., Leten, J., Liss Lymer, B., Schneider, K. and Ward, R. (2020) 'Unpacking water governance: a framework for practi- tioners', *Water* 12 (3): 827 <https://doi.org/10.3390/w12030827>.

Johansson, E. and Debrework, E. (2017) *Public–Private Collaboration in Sanitation Markets: Global Scan and Potential for Ethiopia*, USAID Transform WASH

Learning Note, IRC, Addis Ababa <https://www.ircwash.org/sites/default/files/learning_note_-_public-private_collaboration_novemember_2017.pdf>.

Kendall, L. and Snel, M. (2016) *Looking at WASH in Non-Household Settings: WASH Away from the Home Information Guide*, IRC International Water and Sanitation Centre, The Hague <https://www.ircwash.org/sites/default/files/literature_review_wash_away_from_home_web_0.pdf>.

Lattimer, C. and Swithern, S. (2017) *Global Humanitarian Assistance Report 2017*, Development Initiatives, Bristol <https://devinit.org/wp-content/uploads/2017/06/GHA-Report-2017-Full-report.pdf>.

Lee, K. and Dodgson, R. (2000) 'Globalization and cholera: implications for global governance', *Global Governance* 6 (2): 213–36.

Le Seve, M.D. and Mason, N. (2019) *Building Evidence to Inform the Effective Use of Cash and Voucher Assistance in Emergency Sanitation and Hygiene Programming*, Save the Children UK, London <https://www.alnap.org/help-library/building-evidence-to-inform-the-effective-use-of-cash-and-voucher-assistance-in>.

Lloyd, A. (2017) 'Workshop report: moving from humanitarian to sustainable WASH services in the Middle East Region: Amman, Jordan: 19–21st September 2017', World Vision <https://www.wvi.org/sites/default/files/Workshop%20report-%20Moving%20from%20humanitarian%20to%20sustainable%20WASH.pdf>.

Marshall, T. (2015) *Prisoners of Geography: Ten Maps that Explain Everything about the World*, Elliott and Thompson, London.

Mason, N. and Mosello, B. (2016) 'Making humanitarian and development WASH work better together', Overseas Development Institute, London.

Mason, N., Mosello, B., Shah, J. and Grieve, T. (2017) 'Improving the fit between development and humanitarian WASH in protracted crises', conference contribution, Loughborough University <https://hdl.handle.net/2134/31504>.

Mercy Corps (2008) *Water, Sanitation and Hygiene Guidelines*, Mercy Corps, Portland <https://www.humanitarianlibrary.org/resource/water-sanitation-and-hygiene-guidelines-mercycorps-0>.

Mhalu, F.S., Mtango, F.D.E. and Msengi, E. (1984) 'Hospital outbreaks of cholera transmitted through close person-to-person contact', *Lancet* 324 (8394): 82–4 <https://doi.org/10.1016/S0140-6736(84)90250-2>.

Moffa, M., Cronk, R., Padilla, L., Fejfar, D., Dancausse, S. and Bartram, J. (2018) 'A systematic review of environmental health conditions and hygiene behaviors in homeless shelters', *International Journal of Hygiene and Environmental Health* 222 (3): 335–46 <https://doi.org/10.1016/j.ijheh.2018.12.004>.

Moffa, M., Cronk, R., Fejfar, D., Dancausse, S., Padilla, L. and Bartram, J. (2019) 'A systematic scoping review of hygiene behaviors and environmental health conditions in institutional care settings for orphaned and abandoned children', *Science of the Total Environment* 658: 1161–74 <https://doi.org/10.1016/j.scitotenv.2018.12.286>.

Nakamitsu, I., Eziakonwa-Onochie, A., Ging, J. and Ruedas, M. (2017) 'Humanitarian–development nexus: what is the new way of working?', webinar, 26 April <http://www.deliveraidbetter.org/webinars/humanitarian-development-nexus/>.

Naylor, K.A. and Gordon, B. (2020) 'Learning from history: sanitation for prosperity: a blog to accompany the launch of the State of the World's Sanitation report', World Health Organization blog, 19 November <https://www.who.int/news/item/19-11-2020-learning-from-history-sanitation-for-prosperity>.

OCHA (2015) 'Health system on the verge of collapse', *Humanitarian Bulletin Yemen* 6 <https://reliefweb.int/sites/reliefweb.int/files/resources/OCHA_YEMEN_Hum_Bulletin_6_30_Nov.pdf>.

OCHA (2017) *The New Way of Working*, United Nations Office for the Coordination of Humanitarian Affairs, Geneva <https://www.unocha.org/sites/unocha/files/NWOW%20Booklet%20low%20res.002_0.pdf>.

OCHA (2020a) *Global Humanitarian Overview 2021*, OCHA, Geneva <https://www.unocha.org/global-humanitarian-overview-2021>.

OCHA (2020b) *Humanitarian Needs Overview: Nigeria*, OCHA, New York <https://www.humanitarianresponse.info/sites/www.humanitarianresponse.info/files/documents/files/ocha_nga_humanitarian_needs_overview_december 2020.pdf>.

OCHA (2021) *Humanitarian Needs Overview: Yemen*, OCHA, New York <https://reliefweb.int/sites/reliefweb.int/files/resources/Yemen_HNO_2021_Final.pdf>.

ODI (2015) *Doing Cash Differently: How Cash Transfers Can Transform Humanitarian Aid*, Overseas Development Institute, London <https://www.odi.org/sites/odi.org.uk/files/odi-assets/publications-opinion-files/9828.pdf>.

OECD (2010) *Managing Water for All: An OECD Perspective on Pricing and Financing. Key Messages for Policy Matters*, Organisation for Economic Co-operation and Development, Paris.

OECD (2020) *States of Fragility 2020*, OECD Publishing, Paris <https://doi.org/10.1787/ba7c22e7-en>.

Ramesh, A., Blanchet, K., Ensink, J.H.J. and Roberts, B. (2015) 'Evidence on the effectiveness of water, sanitation, and hygiene (WASH) interventions on health outcomes in humanitarian crises: a systematic review', *PloS One* 10 (9): e0124688 <https://doi.org/10.1371/journal.pone.0124688>.

Rammal, I. (2019) 'Water sector resilience', paper presented at the World Water Week 2019, Stockholm, 25 August.

Ruan, S., Wang, W. and Levin, S.A. (2005) 'The effect of global travel on the spread of SARS', *Mathematical Biosciences and Engineering* 3 (1): 205–18 <https://doi.org/10.3934/mbe.2006.3.205>.

Sadoff, C., Borgomeo, E. and de Waal, D. (2017) *Turbulent Waters: Pursuing Water Security in Fragile Contexts*, World Bank Group, Washington DC <https://openknowledge.worldbank.org/bitstream/handle/10986/26207/W16005.pdf?sequence=2&isAllowed=y>.

Save the Children (2019) *WASH in Temporary Learning Centres: A Conversation Around Key Indicators*, Save the Children, London.

Saywell, D. and Crocker, J. (2019) 'Process learning on partnerships: building functioning research and practice organizational relationships', *Waterlines* 38 (1): 3–19 <https://doi.org/10.3362/1756-3488.18-00014>.

Singh, S. and Bisht, A. (2014) 'Environmental management in mass gatherings: a case study of Maha Kumbh Mela 2013 at Prayag, India', *International Journal for Innovative Research in Science and Technology* 1 (7): 107–115.

Smith, E. (2018a) 'Opportunity driving change in global development sectors', Devex, 17 July [online] <https://www.devex.com/news/sponsored/opportunity-driving-change-in-global-development-sectors-93085>.

Smith, E. (2018b) 'Business experience will be valuable for development professionals of the future', Devex, 30 July [online] <https://www.devex.com/news/sponsored/business-experience-will-be-valuable-for-development-professionals-of-the-future-93151>.

Snel, M. (2015) 'Water, sanitation and disabilities', IRC International Water and Sanitation Centre, 10 June [online] <https://www.ircwash.org/news/wash-and-disabilities>.

Snel, M. (2018) *Creating Sustainable WASH Programmes: A Compilation of Lessons Learned in Five Countries: Afghanistan, Iraq, Jordan, Lebanon and Syria*, World Vision <https://www.wvi.org/clean-water-sanitation-and-hygiene-wash/publication/creating-sustainable-wash-programmes-compilation>.

Snel, M. and Verhoeven, J. (2016) *Lessons Learnt from WASH Action Research with Practitioners in Four Countries: Bangladesh, Ethiopia, Ghana and Uganda*, IRC and WASH Alliance International, The Hague.

Snel, M., Bostoen, K. and Biran, A. (2015) 'Strengthening the role of WASH and disabilities in Bangladesh', paper prepared for the 38th Water, Engineering and Development Centre (WEDC), International Conference, Loughborough University <https://www.ircwash.org/sites/default/files/snel-2222.pdf>.

Snel, M., Shordt, K. and Mooijman, A. (eds) (2004) *Symposium Proceedings & Framework for Action: School Sanitation & Hygiene Education Symposium. The Way Forward: Construction Is Not Enough*, IRC International Water and Sanitation Centre, Delft <https://www.ircwash.org/sites/default/files/Snel-2004-School.pdf>.

SNV and IRC (2013) *Study on Menstrual Management in Uganda*, Netherlands Development Organization (SNV) and IRC International Water and Sanitation Centre, Delft <https://www.ircwash.org/sites/default/files/menstrual_management_study-report_0.pdf>.

Sorensen, N. and Snel, M. (2020) 'The new reality: perspectives on future integrated WASH', *Waterlines* 39 (4): 277–92 <https://doi.org/10.3362/1756-3488.20-00007>.

Sphere Association (2018) *The Sphere Handbook: Humanitarian Charter and Minimum Standards in Humanitarian Response*, 4th edn, Sphere Association, Geneva <https://www.spherestandards.org/handbook>.

Sphere Project (2011) *The Sphere Project: Humanitarian Charter and Minimum Standards in Humanitarian Response*, 3rd edn, Sphere Project, Geneva <https://en.calameo.com/read/004354656752543f6bb9f>.

SWA (2020a) 'Building blocks', Sanitation and Water for All, 31 January <https://www.sanitationandwaterforall.org/about/our-work/priority-areas/building-blocks>.

SWA (2020b) *SWA Report on the 2020 Finance Ministers' Meetings*, SWA, New York <https://www.sanitationandwaterforall.org/sites/default/files/2021-02/53396_29%20-%20SWA%20FMM%20report%20EN_print_1.pdf>.

Tobin, K. (2020) 'If not now, when? WASH is critical to achieving the SDGs, especially in context of COVID-19', WASH Matters, WaterAid, 6 July <https://washmatters.wateraid.org/blog/wash-critical-to-sdgs-especially-in-context-of-covid-19>.

UNHCR (n.d.) 'UNHCR WASH technical designs for refugee settings', United Nations High Commissioner for Refugees, Geneva <https://wash.unhcr.org/wash-technical-designs/>.

UNHCR (2016) *UNHCR WASH Equipment Specifications*, UNHCR, Geneva <https://wash.unhcr.org/download/unhcr-wash-equipment-specifications/>.

UNHCR (2019) *Global Trends: Forced Displacement in 2018*, UNHCR, Geneva <https://www.unhcr.org/5d08d7ee7.pdf>.

UNHCR and UNICEF (2020) 'Blueprint for joint action: briefing paper', UNHCR and UNICEF, New York <https://www.unicef.org/media/85846/file/Briefing%20paper.pdf>.

UNICEF (2016) *Strategy for Water, Sanitation and Hygiene 2016–2030*, Programme Division, United Nations Children's Fund, New York.

UNICEF (2019) *Water Under Fire. Volume 1: Emergencies, Development and Peace in Fragile and Conflict-Affected Contexts*, UNICEF, New York.

UNICEF (2020) 'A joint letter from the water, sanitation and hygiene (WASH) actors in Yemen', UNICEF, 16 June <https://www.unicef.org/yemen/press-releases/joint-letter-water-sanitation-and-hygiene-wash-actors-yemen>.

UNICEF and WHO (2015) *Water, Sanitation and Hygiene in Health Care Facilities: Status in Low- and Middle-Income Countries and Way Forward*, UNICEF and World Health Organization, Geneva <https://reliefweb.int/report/world/water-sanitation-and-hygiene-health-care-facilities-status-low-and-middle-income>.

UNICEF and WHO (2018) *Drinking Water, Sanitation and Hygiene in Schools: Global Baseline Report 2018*, United Nations, New York.

UNICEF and WHO (2020) *State of the World's Sanitation: An Urgent Call to Transform Sanitation for Better Health, Environments, Economies and Societies*, UNICEF and WHO, New York.

United Nations (2016) 'One humanity: shared responsibility: report of the Secretary-General for the World Humanitarian Summit', United Nations, New York <https://agendaforhumanity.org/sites/default/files/Secretary-General's%20Report%20for%20WHS.pdf>.

United Nations (2018) *The Global Compact on Refugees*, United Nations, New York <https://www.unhcr.org/uk/the-global-compact-on-refugees.html>.

VOICE and CONCORD (2012) 'VOICE – CONCORD position paper: linking relief rehabilitation and development (LRRD): towards a more joined up approach enhancing resilience and impact', CONCORD and Voluntary Organisation in Cooperation in Emergencies, Brussels <https://reliefweb.int/sites/reliefweb.int/files/resources/VOICE%20CONCORD%20position%20paper%20Linking%20Relief%20Rehabilitation%20and%20Development-July%202012.pdf>.

WASH Alliance International: Accelerating WASH (n.d.) 'Welcome to the FIETS sustainability portal' <https://wash-alliance.org/our-approach/sustainability/>.

Weber, N. (2019) 'Developing and applying a conceptual evaluation framework for "WaSH FIT" in health care facilities', paper presented at the UNC Water and Health conference, 'Where Science Meets Policy', University of North Carolina, Chapel Hill, 10 October <https://waterinstitute.unc.edu/conferences/waterandhealth2019/>.

WHO (2006) *The World Health Report 2006: Working Together for Health*, World Health Organization, Geneva.

WHO (2015) 'Health system in Yemen close to collapse', *Bulletin of the World Health Organization* 93 (10): 670–1 <https://doi.org/10.2471/BLT.15.021015>.

WHO (2017) *UN-Water Global Analysis and Assessment of Sanitation and Drinking-Water (GLAAS) 2017 Report: Financing Universal Water, Sanitation and Hygiene under the Sustainable Development Goals*, WHO, Geneva.

WHO and UNICEF (2016) *Global Action Plan: Water, Sanitation and Hygiene (WASH) in Health Care Facilities*, World Health Organization and United Nations Children's Fund, Geneva <https://www.wssc.org/media/resources/global-action-plan-water-sanitation-and-hygiene-wash-health-care-facilities>.

WHO and UNICEF (2019) *WASH in Health Care Facilities: Global Baseline Report 2019*, WHO and UNICEF, Geneva <https://apps.who.int/iris/bitstream/handle/10665/311620/9789241515504-eng.pdf?ua=1>.

WHO and UNICEF (2020) 'Water, sanitation, hygiene, and waste management for SARS-CoV-2, the virus that causes COVID-19: interim guidance', WHO and UNICEF, Geneva <https://www.who.int/publications/i/item/WHO-2019-nCoV-IPC-WASH-2020.4>.

World Bank (2020) 'World Bank expands support for basic service delivery to Rohingya and local communities in Cox's Bazar', press release, World Bank Group, 19 November <https://www.worldbank.org/en/news/press-release/2020/11/19/world-bank-expands-support-for-basic-service-delivery-to-rohingya-and-local-communities-in-coxs-bazar>.

World Bank Group (2014) *Myanmar: Ending Poverty and Boosting Shared Prosperity in a Time of Transition*, World Bank Group, Yangon, Myanmar <http://documents1.worldbank.org/curated/en/871761468109465157/pdf/930500CSD0P150070Box385388B00OUO090.pdf>.

World Bank, ICRC, and UNICEF (2021) *Joining Forces to Combat Protracted Crises: Humanitarian and Development Support for Water Supply and Sanitation Providers in the Middle East and North Africa*, World Bank, Washington DC <https://www.icrc.org/en/document/joining-forces-secure-water-and-sanitation-protracted-crises>.

World Vision (2017) 'Sesame Street, World Vision partnership expands to 11 countries with lifesaving hygiene lessons', World Vision, 13 October <https://www.worldvision.org/about-us/media-center/sesame-street-partnership-expands>.

World Vision (2019) 'Solid waste management in refugee camps in Jordan', ReliefWeb, 18 November <https://reliefweb.int/report/jordan/policy-paper-solid-waste-management-refugee-camps-jordan>.

World Vision (2020) 'Macro-catchment construction: alleviating the threat of both flash flooding and water shortages in western Afghanistan', World Vision Afghanistan <https://www.wvi.org/publications/brochure/afghanistan/macro-catchment-construction>.

Yates, T., Allen, J., Joseph, M.L. and Lantagne, D. (2017a) *Short-term WASH Interventions in Emergency Response: A Systematic Review*, 3ie Systematic Review 33, International Initiative for Impact Evaluation (3ie), London.

Yates, T., Allen, J., Joseph, M.L. and Lantagne, D. (2017b) *Wash Interventions in Disease Outbreak Response*, Oxfam GB: Humanitarian Evidence Programme, Oxford <https://www.alnap.org/system/files/content/resource/files/main/wash-systematic-review.pdf>.

Index

Printed in the USA
CPSIA information can be obtained
at www.ICGtesting.com
JSHW012017140824
68134JS00025B/2461